LEADERSHIP,
AUTHORITY,
AND
POWER SHARING

LEADERSHIP, AUTHORITY, AND POWER SHARING

Henry Clay Lindgren, Ph.D.
Professor of Psychology
San Francisco State University

ROBERT E. KRIEGER PUBLISHING COMPANY
MALABAR, FLORIDA
1982

Original edition 1982
(Based upon "Effective Leadership in Human Relations")

(Substantial portions of this book appeared in *Effective Leadership in Human Relations*, by the same author, published by Hermitage House, New York, in 1954.)

Printed and Published by
ROBERT E. KRIEGER PUBLISHING CO., INC.
Krieger Drive
Malabar, FL 32950

Library of Congress Cataloging in Publication Data

Lindgren, Henry Clay, 1914-
   Leadership, authority, and managerial power-sharing.

   Bibliography: p.
   Includes index.
   1. Social psychology—United States.   2. Leadership.
3. Management.   4. Social groups.   I. Title.
HM271.L54   302   81-18644
ISBN 0-89874-251-X   AACR2

Preface

For more than thirty years I have, as a social psychologist, observed the interaction between individuals in positions of leadership or authority and those they administer, manage, advise, direct, or otherwise try to influence. What I have seen convinces me that leaders and other authority figures—I shall use the two terms interchangeably—have an especially difficult time in this country. Elsewhere, being authority figure does not seem to be as stressful. In other countries, the individual who occupies a position of recognized status is reasonably certain of a degree of acceptance and cooperation from those he leads or supervises. Outside America, people seem to recognize that leaders are necessary—and are more willing to give them the benefit of the doubt until they prove themselves unworthy or inadequate. The mood of America, especially of its young, was tersely but eloquently expressed by a bumper strip I recently saw on a Datsun: "Question authority!"

In America, we seem unsure of whether leaders are really necessary and hence must repeatedly put them to the test. A person who steps into a position of authority therefore finds himself in the line of fire. If he has been appointed, he may discover that as a representative of top management or "the establishment," he has fallen heir to an accumulated backlog of unresolved dissatisfactions. His attempts to carry out the organization's program thus meets with resistance or apathy. If he has been elected by a majority, those in the losing minority feel committed to an adversary stance regarding his attempts to bring harmony to the membership. And in either event, the leader often finds himself unable to depend on those from whom he would expect support and cooperation. Most people in this country would agree—some of them reluctantly—that leaders are necessary, but they also seem to think that they are expendable. Indeed, it is a continuing miracle that so many of our leaders survive their abrasive experiences and that some, in fact, are the stronger for it and carry out their duties successfully and with style.

These successes should not blind us to the fact that most leaders also fail. Some fail only occasionally, some fail in the sense that they are but partially successful, and some are chronic failures. Even those who are most successful are well acquainted with failure and succeed only because they persist, forging ahead in spite of setbacks and disappointments.

It is my belief that people in authority generally do not know why they have failed. Most of them, to be sure, know some of the reasons but nevertheless remain unaware of the more significant causes—those that involve the psychology of people's behavior toward and with persons in authority. It is my conviction that if individuals in positions of authority had a better understanding of those dynamics, they would be spared a great deal of puzzlement and anxiety and would be able to deal both directly and successfully with the potential causes of failure. This all calls for a style of group management which is different from that traditionally displayed by persons in authority, for Americans today seem unwilling or unable to respond to traditional strategies of leadership.

It is the aim of this book to shed some light on factors that cause problems for administrators and other types of leaders—factors that, being psychological, are usually overlooked. Chief among them is a pervasive hostility toward persons possessing power, especially toward those directly in charge. This hostility ordinarily expresses itself in the form of resistance, both passive and active. To illustrate these problems, I shall present some examples in anecdotal form, of typical situations faced by persons in authority. I shall indicate the reasons why these difficulties occur and suggest strategies for dealing with them. The anecdotes are creations of my imagination, and any resemblance to actual persons or events is coincidental. This does not prevent them from being any less real, for the conflicts and frustrations they portray are drawn from life itself. The people who figure in these examples could be anyone, not excepting the reader and the author.

The approaches I have used in discussing problems of leadership and authority are not original with me. The list of those from whom I have borrowed is long. Furthermore, some of the ideas and concepts I have collected over the last three decades have become so much a part of my philosophy and leadership style that I no longer know where I got them. I can, however, identify a few of those whose influence on my thinking has been most marked: Rensis Likert, Daniel Katz, Ronald Lippitt, Frederick Herzberg, Chris Argyris, Norman R.F. Maier, Kurt Lewin, Carl R. Rogers, Donald Snygg, Arthur S. Combs, F.J. Roethlisberger, and Marvin E. Shaw.

It is important to include a few words about the use of "he" and "him" in this book. Many writers these days use the forms "she and he" and "him and her" in reference to individuals who play certain roles, such as "leader" or "executive," that may be taken either by women or by men. It is argued that the use of the two pronouns recognizes that there is no difference between the sexes either in their ability or in their right to exercise the functions and skills of these roles. The difficulty that results from this usage, however, is that the repeated appearance of both pronouns creates an awkwardness in the flow of ideas and distracts the reader who is trying to understand what the writer is saying. It is in recognition of this problem that I elected to stay with the more conventional "he/him," when discussing an individual of unspecified sex, instead of the cumbersome "he and she" or "her and him." Thus the leaders or authority figures I describe and analyze may be either women or men. In any event, I fully support the idea that the ability or the right to perform as a leader is not specific to the male sex.

Henry Clay Lindgren
San Francisco State University

January, 1981

Contents

CHAPTER ONE

What Did I Do to Deserve All This Hostility?

It was perfectly plain to Edith that her husband was out of sorts. She had been aware of it from the moment he had come home from the office.

She was usually in the kitchen preparing dinner when Howard came from work, and he would usually let her know when he came in by shouting "'Allo, keed!" like a phony Frenchman, or "Are you theah?" with an affected British accent. But today she had only heard the front door open and close. After a while she said: "Is that you, Howard?"

The only reply was a grunt. As she peeked around the corner into the living room, he was already immersed in the evening paper.

During dinner he said very little. Howard was not what you would call a brilliant conversationalist at the dinner table, but he could be depended on for the more routine questions: "How did it go at the clinic today?" or "What's the latest from the Potter Valley Protective Society?"—his pet name for the three retired couples across the street who took a militant stance on every issue, large or small. But tonight he seemed lost in thought and hardly said a word.

Edith watched him closely, to see if he was getting one of the digestive upsets he had periodically. But his appetite seemed good, and he even had seconds on dessert.

Once Edith asked him: "Everything OK at work, dear?" He looked at her rather sharply for a moment, and then said, "Fine, fine," and went on stirring his coffee absently.

Edith had planned after dinner to strip the varnish off a table she had bought at a garage sale, and Howard had said that he would help her. In the past, when they had worked together on such chores, Howard would talk about the projects he was working on at the office, what he had said to Mr. Ortiz and what Mr. Ortiz had said to him. Over the years, Edith had acquired a fair grasp of the main currents in office politics and could be counted on for insightful analyses and comments. But tonight Howard worked silently and not too efficiently, as though his mind were elsewhere. When he had dropped the scraper for the third time, Edith decided to call a halt. Gently but firmly she took the tool from his hands and headed him in the direction of the basement.

"You go down and work with your fishing tackle," she suggested. "I'll be down shortly."

Howard grinned sheepishly and headed on down the basement stairs.

A half hour later, Edith came down with her knitting basket and seated herself on the high stool near the work bench, just under the light. She noticed that Howard had taken out his reels but hadn't done much else. She unfurled the sweater she was working on, got her needles going, and then said:

"O.K. Tell Mother all about it."

Howard seemed surprised.

"Tell Mother about what?"

"Something's on your mind. Something's eating you. I've known it ever since you came home tonight. You'll feel better after you tell me about it."

"Oh." He seemed embarrassed.

Edith said nothing. Just went on knitting as though getting the sweater done was the most important business of the moment.

Howard fiddled with one of his reels and then said, impatiently:

"I feel like a fool talking to you about this. Probably because it was all my fault. I should have remembered that Ed is awfully sensitive."

Edith said nothing but she thought: "Ed again, eh?"

When Howard had gone to work for the Company six years ago, Ed had been a sort of father to him—showed him the ropes, kept him informed on interoffice politics, and gave him some good pointers on how to build up his sales production. Ed always said that the very last thing he wanted out of life was to manage, what with the headaches and all that went with the job, but since Howard had been made sales manager six months ago, Ed had been acting very strangely. No doubt about it; he just wasn't the same person.

Howard continued.

"I had to speak to Ed about the Acme Tool account. The Old Man wanted to be sure that they got the plush treatment. I only wanted to convey the Old Man's ideas to Ed, but I never got a chance. As soon as I mentioned 'Acme' to Ed, he got as red as a turkey gobbler and said that if I didn't like the way he was handling the Acme account, I could jolly well give it to somebody else. And then he just got up and walked out of the office."

"His own office?" asked Edith, surprised.

"No. My office. I had asked him to come in to discuss the matter with him."

Howard started to take one of the reels apart but put it down again.

"I guess today was really 'my day.'" he went on. "You know the trouble I've had with the steno pool. I can't for the life of me figure out why it takes sometimes forty-eight hours to get a letter back after it's been dictated. When I was just a hotshot salesman, I used to kid around with Ollie and she'd get the pool to perform wonders for me. But now she calls me 'Mr. Galvin," and when I ask her to give a job a special push, she says: 'You know we always do our best, Mr. Galvin.' Now frankly I just question that. For example, four of the girls went out for their coffee break at 10 o'clock this morning, leaving Ollie to hold down the desk. Ollie herself left at 10:30, leaving no one. The rest of the gang sauntered in at 10:45, with Ollie joining them at five minutes to 11. Now what kind of business is that? The worst of it is that this has been going on for *months!* I had the feeling that they were staying out awfully long, but I didn't know how bad it really was till I did this time check on them this morning."

Edith looked up from her knitting. "Don't keep me on tenterhooks," she said. "What did you tell them?"

Howard looked sheepish.

"That's just the trouble. I didn't tell them anything. On the one hand, I felt mad as hell about it, but on the other hand, I had this big report for the Board. I had the stuff just about ready and I wanted Ollie to start her girls on it this afternoon. I couldn't very well jaw them out one minute and then the next minute ask them to highball this special job through. So I seethed and simmered for a while till I got control of myself and then called Ollie in to tell her the glad news about the special report. When I got through going over the material I asked her how long it would take her to get the job out. Now I know damn good and well that in the days when I was just a salesman she would have said the day after tomorrow. Wednesday. Wednesday at the *latest.* But do you know what she said? She said *Friday!*"

Howard turned away from the bench as he said this. His hands were clenched and his mouth was a grim line.

Edith was not knitting now. She was watching Howard and there was a worried look on her face. She waited for him to go on.

"Well, I took that pretty well, I think. I'm learning. You can't ram things down people's throats, even though they deserve it sometimes. I just looked Ollie in the eye and said: 'Ollie, this is a special job. A *very* special job. It has to be done by 4 p.m. Wednesday to be ready for the Board meeting on Thursday morning. I'm expecting it Wednesday.'

"Well, she sort of stammered and looked down at her feet and said something about it being necessary to let other work go in order to get the report out Wednesday. All I said was: 'That's between you and the rest of the men in the office, Ollie. If you can get them to go along with a delayed schedule, O.K. But I'm expecting this report Wednesday.'"

Edith smiled and picked up her knitting again.

"If I know Ollie, she'll get your report to you on time and keep up with her other work besides," she commented. "I think you handled *that* one pretty well."

"Meaning I didn't handle Ed very well?" Howard asked with wry amusement. "I suppose you're right. Oh, I suppose I did the right thing with Ollie, all right. But that's not what worries me. What really gets under my skin is her attitude. How can anybody change so much in six months? I don't get it."

Edith frowned, ripped out the last two rows, and then started over.

"Maybe *you're* the one has changed," she suggested.

Howard chewed on a pine shaving absently.

"You could be right," he admitted. "They say there's nothing that changes a person like being promoted. Of course, I always thought I would be an exception. But *you* should be able to answer that one. Do *you* think I have changed?"

Edith looked up from her knitting and started to meet his challenge with a light laugh, then changed her mind and grew serious.

"We-ell," she said slowly, "now that I think of it, you *do* take things a lot more seriously than you used to. I think you worry more about things. And you don't spend as much time down here as you used to," she added, indicating the workshop with a sweep of her hand.

"There's no doubt that I have more on my mind and that I spend more time working at the office or here at home, but I mean, have I *really* changed?"

Edith stopped knitting and thought a minute.

"No," she said, "I don't think you have. But maybe I'm too close to you to tell. Or maybe you haven't changed with me so much as with other people. How about people *away* from the office?"

Howard chewed thoughtfully on his pine chip for a minute and then spit it out impatiently.

"Oh, hell, how should I know?" he exploded. "You can imagine all kinds of things if you go looking for trouble in your life. Now take what happened last night at the church."

Edith nodded. "Maybelle told me that there was quite an exciting meeting."

Howard grinned in spite of his irritation.

"Tell me her version after I tell you mine," he said. "As you know, I am the chairman of the Every-Member-Canvass Committee, and we're awfully worried about raising that whopping budget all you parishioners voted in last month."

"Don't forget, you voted for it, too," Edith reminded him.

"I know, but that was before I knew I was going to have to collect it," Howard said, ruefully. "You know, last year the Committee was ten per cent short of the goal. In fact, we've missed our budget by ten to twenty per cent every year for the last five. Well, one of the reasons I was willing to take the job was that I saw a chance to do something for the church that was really in my line. There's not too much difference between raising money for a church budget and running a sales campaign. They're both selling jobs. So I convened my committee and gave them my pitch. I told them that I for one felt that the increased budget was a challenge and not a liability and that there were a number of ways that were very effective when it came to raising money that we hadn't even tried yet. And I gave as an example the trick of listing incomes on a rising scale, together with suggested pledges for each level. The Community Chest uses this approach and apparently it works pretty well. Then I sat back and waited for the committee's reaction."

"From what Maybelle said, the committee didn't take your suggestions lying down," Edith said.

"That is the understatement of the week," grinned Howard. "I had hardly finished when Mr. Whitcomb creaked to his feet and said that *he* had voted against the increased budget, just as he had voted against every budget for the last ten years, and that if anybody wanted *his* opinion as to why we couldn't make our quota it was because the budget was too high.

"Then I began to realize that I had put my foot in it, that I not only had a *real* tough job on my hands, but that I had probably made a bad start by setting the whole committee against me. so I got smart and used a method that Mr. Ortiz told me about when he came back from one of those week-end conferences in the Adirondacks that the top brass has every so often. I just said, 'Does anyone else have anything to say about the job we have before us?'"

"You were really asking for it, weren't you?" murmured Edith.

"You're damn right I was," said Howard. "But it went pretty much as it did in the case Mr. Ortiz told me about. For a half hour most of them followed Mr. Whitcomb's lead and gave me both barrels. The budget was too high, money was getting harder to collect every year, you couldn't get members to go out and solicit, and so forth and so on. I said very little, just jotted down the points as they were made. When they began to repeat themselves at the end of a half hour, I stopped the recital and read off the list I had made. There was a silence after I finished. Then I asked, 'Does anyone have any suggestions as to how we should do this job?' I was *tempted* to say, 'Let's all resign and get a new committee,' but I didn't.

"They looked sort of sheepish at that, and Joe Coombs said, 'How about some of the plans you were telling us about at the beginning of the meeting?'"

Edith smiled. "Joe's the best man you have on the committee."

"I know," Howard replied. "He tried to object to some of the things they were saying at first, but they had him outnumbered. Well, I thought we were cooking on all burners when Joe asked that question, but it didn't turn out that way. But Joe gave it a good start, because Lou Sutter asked me to give the main gist of my talk again, particularly the part about how we were going to conduct the canvassing. So I ran over the points briefly and then waited for the reaction. I don't know what went wrong, because Old Man Whitcomb struggled to his feet again and objected to listing incomes together with suggested pledges. Joe and Lou disagreed. They thought it was a good idea. The first thing I knew, a good, knock-down argument was in progress with Joe and Lou on one side and Mr. Whitcomb and the rest of

the committee on the other. I finally had to step in and bring it to a halt. I
wanted to end the meeting with something constructive, so I suggested that
we look over the collection of printed folders that I had with me that were
used by other churches in their every-member canvasses. The committee
agreed, but I don't think that anybody was very happy with the meeting as
we broke up."

As Howard stopped, Edith said: "Well, it sounds as though you had an
exciting evening, but I don't see that your meeting has much to do with
what we were talking about a while back."

Howard was thoughtful.

"Well it *does*, sort of," he maintained, "because the feeling I had as the
meeting broke up last night was that they blamed *me* for the mess we had
got into, and as I thought of the trouble I had with Ed and Ollie today, it
somehow made me think of last night. I can't help thinking," he went on,
"that all three of these things are kind of related..."

                    *   *   *

We have presented this account about Howard Galvin and his problems
for several reasons. For one thing, we wanted to present a glimpse into the
life of a man who is becoming an effective leader. Too many people in
positions of leadership or authority accept their responsibilities on a
superficial basis and operate on a day-to-day basis, without probing very
deeply into the nature of the problems that confront them.

Perhaps there are some leaders who "get the feel" of the human relations
involved rather easily and perhaps do not need to do the soul-searching
that Howard is doing, but most of us who are leaders, or who are becoming
leaders, need to do more soul-searching and self-analysis, rather than less,
if we are to become more effective. Otherwise, our ability to handle new
situations becomes stereotyped and awkward, with resulting difficulties in
working with people. This, in turn, leads to an increasing use of power-
and-pressure tactics, the old and familiar standby of ineffective authority
figures for generations.

Another reason we have used the story of Howard and his difficulties as
our opening gambit in this discussion is that we wanted to illustrate the
presence of what we feel is an important but largely unrecognized factor in
the relations between leaders and group members, between persons with
supervisory jobs and their subordinates. This factor is *hostility*.

By hostility we mean a wide variety of attitudes, feelings, and behavior
that have a certain basic similarity in that they are all ways of expressing
resistance, antagonism, opposition, and rejection. It is in this broad,
general sense that we shall use the term *hostility* throughout this book.
The origins of the word *hostility* go back to ancient days. It is related to
word roots in Latin, Greek, and other Indo-European languages that mean
stranger or *outsider*. Therefore, the kinds of feelings or emotional states

that we call hostility are the ones that are aroused by the presence of something or someone strange, something that is outside our way of doing things, something that is different. Consequently we react by wanting to attack the strange person or thing or to defend ourselves against it. In any case, we stubbornly resist going along with it. At times, hostility helps us to protect ourselves from being injured or exploited, but at other times, it interferes with our relations with others, keeps us from being cooperative and helpful, and may actually stand in the way of our participation in situations and events that could work out to our personal advantage.

Hostility expresses itself in an endless variety of ways. Strikes, punishment, sabotage, riots, revenge, shouted insults, and warfare are some of the more obvious and more violent forms, but it also expresses itself subtly through apathy and boredom, carelessness, absenteeism, spoilage and wastage, inattention, inefficiency, lowered productivity, expressions of irritation, and the like. Most of the time we are not consciously aware of being hostile, nor are we always aware when those about us are expressing hostility. What usually happens is that we react to each other's hostility with *counter*-hostility without even knowing what we are doing. At best, we may be aware of a feeling of discomfort and impatience or that there is something we do not like. Howard Galvin's reaction is of the latter type. When he comes home, his wife is aware that something is bothering him, although he is only half conscious of it. It is not until later, when he goes over the events of the last twenty-four hours, that he finally catches a glimpse of what has really been going on between him and the people with whom he works.

As leaders or authority figures (and everyone performs such functions at one time or another), we inevitably have to deal with the veiled or open hostility of subordinates. When this occurs, we usually are concerned with the *visible* evidence of resistance, resentment, and other forms of hostility, as though people's *actions* were the chief problem. It usually does not occur to us to consider the underlying causes of the behavior we are experiencing, partly because we are busy defending ourselves against attack or are casting about for ways to make our attempts at direction and supervision more attractive and acceptable. And should anyone suggest that we should take stock of what is going on, we might respond, impatiently, by saying: "Look, this job is tough enough without making it any more complicated. Let's just deal with the problem at hand and not waste time and energy in fantasies and speculations."

Thus we allow ourselves to become prisoners of the immediate situation and keep plugging away, using the same old ineffective methods again and again, wondering why our subordinates do not respond as they should.

All persons in positions of authority or leadership do not fall into this trap, of course. There have always been a handful who have been able to sense the causes of resistance and resentment and have been able to take steps to deal with them intelligently, but today, thanks to the research of behavioral scientists in the fields of social psychology and group processes, there are more people in authority positions who have developed an understanding of the psychological forces underlying group behavior. These leaders are persons who have developed more than the usual amount of skill in human relations. Not all of them can translate their understanding of people into so many words, but the way in which they go about their business as leaders indicates a very broad, deep, and sensitive feeling for the forces and conditions that lie behind the façade of everyday behavior.

We have tried to describe such a leader in our story of Howard Galvin. He is not a leader who has "arrived" but he *is* one who is "arriving." We see him at his best when he deals with Ollie. Ollie has always occupied a spot lower than his on the office totem pole, and he is very likely more comfortable in playing a leadership role with her. Nevertheless, her veiled hostility gets under his skin, and he longs for the easier, friendlier relationship they had before he moved up to a higher spot on the totem pole. He is not quite ready to accept the feeling of partial isolation that often goes with leadership.

Howard's encounter with Ed will have to be written off as a failure. Well, perhaps, not exactly written off, because there *are* some things that he could learn from the incident, provided he is willing to continue his rigorous soul-searching. For example, why did he ask Ed to come to *his* office? Wouldn't it have been more politic to have gone to Ed's? Does this mean that where Ed is concerned, Howard feels more comfortable and secure meeting him in his *own* ground? Does Howard feel a little guilty about being Ed's boss?

His relations with Ed are far more complex than his relations with Ollie. When he first came to the office, Ed displayed a kind of fatherly interest in him. During the intervening years, Howard had grown in experience and status to a point equal to that of the older man. And now he was Ed's boss. For Howard, supervising Ed was a little like having to supervise his own father. Who, then, could blame him for feeling a little awkward and tense in his relations toward a man who had once treated him like a son and whose boss he now was? And who could blame Ed for having mixed feelings about seeing Howard, his own protege, placed in a position of authority over him?

Perhaps if Howard had not had this feeling of awkwardness and tenseness about Ed, he would not have had Ed come to his office in the first place. He would have gone to Ed's office. Then there was the information that he had to communicate to Ed. No one really likes to be a message-carrier for the boss. Actually, Howard would have felt happier if he had been permitted to handle matters his own way, which would have been to trust Ed in handling the Acme account. After all, Ed knew his way around. Yet the boss's orders were pretty explicit, and he felt that he had no choice but to deliver them as directed.

The situation, to use a popular phrase, was loaded with dynamite. Both men were aware of its potential dangers, yet neither did anything to halt the course of events. Judging them from our safe and comfortable distance, we can easily see that Howard must bear the greater responsibility for what happened. As the person in authority, he had greater control over the conditions under which the discussion of the Acme account would take place. Furthermore, any additional moves to improve the worsened relations between Ed and him must be his to initiate.

Howard's encounter with the Every-Member-Canvass Committee will have to be put down as a draw. The inconclusive results are due to many factors, not the least of which is the atmosphere of disunity, general confusion, and fairly open hostility that characterizes the group. Howard's opening statements were ill-conceived and badly handled. In his eagerness to get the job underway, he completely misjudged the members of the committee and their attitudes toward the task at hand. But he recovered himself in good order and would have saved the day if it had not been for Mr. Whitcomb's generally negative feelings about the whole idea of fund-raising. (Indeed, one sometimes wonders why so many Mr. Whitcombs show up on committees whose purposes and functions they so completely reject.)

And so the meeting ended in an impasse. What will come of future meetings will depend very largely on Howard's skill in getting people with such diverse views to agree on the functions and goals of the committee and to work together with reasonable harmony. His task is a difficult one, but no more difficult than that of many other committee chairmen who have been assigned unreasonable tasks that have to be accomplished with the aid of unreasonable committees.

If Howard succeeds in this assignment, it will be partly because he has developed a clear idea of where the hostility lies and what arouses it. In other words, he will learn how to avoid arousing hostility and how to hold it in check or reduce it when it rises to the point where it interferes with the progress of the group. Another ability that will stand him in good stead will be his ability to sense and control the *level of anxiety* in the group. We shall have more to say about both hostility and anxiety in the next few chapters.

Howard shows good promise as a leader. He is already aware that there are factors that are common to the three incidents he describes. If he develops into a really effective leader, in the broadest sense of the word, one of the things that he will learn is that the leader in our society must be prepared to be the target for many forms of hostile behavior. He will be able to explain some of these as reactions to his own awkwardness or insensitivity, but much hostility he experiences will be *unearned*—part of what goes with the position of leader, authority figure, or supervisor. Because it is unearned, he may not recognize it as hostility, but if he is perceptive, he will recognize it for what it is and deal with it appropriately.

CHAPTER TWO

Why Hostility Makes Us Anxious

In our introductory chapter, we tried to show how hostility plays such a large part in the relationship between subordinates or group members and persons who perform the functions of leadership.

In this chapter, we shall attempt to probe into some of our reactions to hostility. We shall be concerned with why we are so uncomfortable when we become the targets for hostile attitudes or acts. Why, for example, did Howard get upset at Ed's outburst? After all, he *knows* that Ed is sensitive about his promotion and he knows that Ed is not interested in replacing him as sales manager. If he knows these things, why does he let Ed "get under his skin"?

And there is the incident with Ollie. Howard won *that* round by refraining from saying the wrong things and by saying the right ones. He has every right to feel good about the results of that encounter. Yet he is disturbed. Again, why?

Much of what is disturbing Howard is what psychologists since the Age of Freud have been calling *anxiety*. Like hostility, anxiety is an emotion that is expressed in many forms. It may, for example, be sensed as a vague feeling of dread or apprehension or as a persistent, bothersome tension.

The Neo-Freudian psychiatrist, Harry Stack Sullivan, theorized that anxiety is the product of disturbances in interpersonal relations. It appears in its most straightforward form in infants. Sullivan observed that infants are strongly affected, both emotionally and physically, by the moods and feelings of their mothers. For example, children commonly develop feeding difficulties and digestive upsets when their mothers are disturbed, angry, depressed, irritated, or disappointed. It does not seeem to matter whether the mother's mood is directly concerned with the child or not. This accounts, at least in part, for the common phenomenon of feeding difficulties, excessive crying, or actual illnesses that occur so often among infants and small children when their families—and hence their mothers—are more than usually disturbed. Violent quarrelling,

11

temporary or permanent loss of a member of the family, moving, family crises, and divorce usually are reflected in infant health or behavior problems. Sullivan called this sensitivity to the emotions and feelings of others *empathy*. We shall have more to say about empathy in a later connection.

As infants become children, they learn to tell the difference between the various situations that cause anxiety. A child discovers, for example, that when his mother is upset, it is not always because she is angry or disappointed with *him*. She may be angry at an older brother or sister. He is still very likely to be anxious when this occurs, but not nearly as anxious as when the anger or disapproval is directed toward him. Normally, he learns how to avoid some of the disapproval (hostility) of his parents by avoiding behavior that brings it on. Such learning comes as the result of many frustrating incidents, whereby the child discovers, by painful degrees, that the way to keep his parents' favor and avoid the experience of anxiety, is to conform to the patterns of behavior that they prescribe for him. There are, of course, many variations on this theme, depending on the nature and personality of the child, the kinds of demands made by the parents, and the occurence of events over which neither parents nor child have much control.

Let us stop at this point and take a look at what we have said about anxiety. We have tried to show that it is aroused when children feel that their parents disapprove of them, that it is a painful emotion, and that it can be avoided or at least reduced when children learn to do what their parents expect of them.

It should be evident from what we have said that developing what we might call *normal anxiety* is very much a part of growing up, because the child who has sufficient *normal* anxiety is going to be concerned about what his parents think of him and is going to modify his conduct and behavior accordingly—to the extent of his ability, of course. (We have to add this proviso, because many parents expect behavior from their children that is far beyond their level of maturity.) Conversely, the child who does *not* have a sufficient degree of normal anxiety will be less concerned about the thoughts and feelings of his parents, and will be concerned instead with what *he* wants to do and not about what *they* want him to do.

Let no one think, however, that most behavior and nonconformity on the part of children is due to a lack of anxiety. Most of it, indeed, is due to an *excess* of anxiety rather than a lack of it. A little anxiety, as we have shown, is a good thing because it helps the child to be sensitive to the needs of others. But *too much* anxiety—what we shall call *neurotic* anxiety—is disturbing. Many children misbehave because they are the victims of an over-abundance of anxiety, brought about by too much pressure, inconsistencies in discipline, conflicting demands, and so forth. And lest parents appear to be too much the villains in this drama, let us hasten to add that parents themselves have to cope with a superabundance of anxiety too, caused by a world that changes too fast, in-laws who do not approve, tensions at work, the rising cost of living, and the like. In short, the inconsistencies of a more or less neurotic world lead to neurotic anxiety and inconsistent behavior on the part of parents, and this in turn leads to neurotic anxiety and inconsistent behavior of the part of children.

But let us return to our search for the basic elements of hostility and their relationship to anxiety.

As children grow and mature, the number of persons who are important to them increases. Af first there is only mother, then both father and mother, then brothers and sisters and playmates. A little later, other adults also begin to assume roles of importance—teachers, neighbors, relatives, policemen, and so forth. As the child develops through the stages of preadolescence and adolescence, he becomes more or less attached to cliques, gangs, and clubs made up of persons his own age. Through these contacts, he develops a growing awareness of the importance of maintaining good relationships with people in general, or, at least, of avoiding unpleasant ones.

At all times, throughout his relations with these significant people, there is a thread of anxiety, sometimes normal and sometimes neurotic. If he is reasonably well accepted and well liked by playmates or friends and if he gets along fairly well with adults, the chances are that his behavior has been governed, at least in part, by normal anxiety—that is, he has been concerned about keeping the good will of others, he has not been insistent on having his own way all the time, he has been reasonably considerate of the feelings of others, and he has conformed, within reason, to what others expected of him.

If his experience has been at all typical, there have been times when he has been hurt or upset by the actions of others. Sometimes this has happened because of real or fancied wrongs suffered at the hands of someone he thought was a good friend. But what has hurt him the most has been the occasional feeling of being rejected by the gang, the clique, or the crowd, for one of the things that he has learned to respect is the power that the group can wield. When his friends have for some reason neglected to include him in their activities or when they have criticized or teased or embarrassed him, his anxieties are likely to rise to painful levels. For this reason, he has learned to be very careful not to run counter to the group. If his friends flock to country-and-western or rock concerts, he must go too. If all the other girls wear sequined sweaters, or leather jackets, or copper bracelets, she must do likewise. If one's friends cut high-school classes and smoke pot, one must fall in line or suffer the ignominy and disgrace of being excluded from their activities. Such rejection is usually underscored by a show of hostility and always arouses anxiety.

One of the most pronouced characteristics of anxiety is the feeling of helplessness that accompanies it. Therefore, when a teenager finds himself being forced to do something which is contrary to the norms and standards of his gang, he feels lost, alone, and helpless. This is one of the reasons why he will go to such great lengths to avoid doing anything that will cut him off from a group that has become so deeply and so personally a part of him. This is also why children and adults alike are so careful about doing anything that will call forth the disapproval of groups or organizations that are psychologically important to them.

*   *   *

Jean Ford bit her lip with exasperation when they nominated Joyce Grow for president of the Suburban Club. If the club only knew what she knew about Joyce, they'd. . . . Well, they wouldn't *really* elect her president. With Joyce as president it would mean that the club would embark on one crusade after another.

Within a month, Jean thought, Joyce would be having the club saving the city from the politicians, or up to their ears writing letters to senators, or attending meetings of the city council. Jean sighed. The Suburban Club had really become a part of her life in the ten years that she had belonged. Almost every one of her friends belonged too. She liked the luncheons and the card parties, and last year they had some really excellent speakers. When she had been the chairman of the program committee, they had arranged for a series of book reviews. That was a good year. They still talked about those reviews and how much they liked them.

But now, if Joyce got to be president, there'd be none of those nice, pleasant meetings. Joyce'd always be stirring up some kind of controversy. . . .

As all this passed through Jean's mind, she heard the president ask if there were any more nominations. She wanted to say, "Yes!" She wanted to get up to her feet and nominate Sheila Way or Evelyn Schluter or any of her other friends. Anyone would be better than Joyce. They'd probably be elected, too. How could anyone really want Joyce as a president? The nominating committee must have been out of their minds.

She heard someone move that the nominations be closed. The motion was seconded, and a moment later, Jean found herself voting with the other members of the club to make Joyce Grow's election unanimous.

*   *   *

Probably there is no one who reads this book who has not been in a similar predicament, who has not had feelings and conflicts similar to Jean's. We may feel strongly opposed to a move that our group is making, yet we are afraid to raise a dissenting voice. Although the chances are very small that we will be excluded from the group merely by speaking out, we are kept firmly in line by the fear of our own anxiety. The group might be a little irritated or impatient with us if we broke into the even pace of its routine with our objections. And they might express their rejection of us by laughing.

It is hard for us to bear the anxiety aroused even by a little hostility, because with this anxiety comes the feeling of desperate helplessness that to some degree is a psychological echo of the way we felt in childhood and infancy when we thought our parents no longer cared for us; for this is very likely how children and even infants feel when they sense the anger and disapproval of their parents.

*   *   *

When Louis Koch asked for a job at the Engine Rebuilding Company, Mr. Kendall, the manager, looked dubious. He was even more skeptical when Louis told him that he had lived all of his twenty-two years on a farm, but had to look for some other kind of work when his back had been injured. Louis claimed to have a lot of experience repairing farm machinery. This wasn't the kind of background that Mr. Kendall usually looked for, but the way things were, he couldn't afford to be choosey. Besides, Louis looked as though he really wanted to work, which was more than you could say for a good two-thirds of the applicants he interviewed.

Mr. Kendall put Louis to work rebuilding generators. The plant was away behind on generators, and for some reason it was harder to keep people in that department. One of these days, Mr. Kendall told himself, he was going to find out why.

Because of a number of problems that came up after he hired Louis, Mr. Kendall forgot all about him until one day about three months later. He happened to be checking over the payroll when he caught sight of Louis' name. But what amazed him was that Louis was drawing the largest paycheck of any of the nonsupervisory employees. Since the plant was operating on a piecework basis, this meant that Louis was turning out a lot more generators than anybody else. This was certainly a surprising performance for a boy only three months off the farm. He decided to look further into the matter.

As soon as he had finished the work at hand, he dropped in to see the foreman of the electrical shop, a solemn Scot named Sandy Buchanan.

"Tell me about this Koch boy, Sandy," he asked.

Sandy pulled at his pipe for a minute before answering.

"He's about as clever a lad with his hands as I've ever had," he replied. "But he's headed for trouble if he stays here."

Mr. Kendall was surprised.

"How so?" he demanded. "He's turning out more production than any man in the shop. I'd say he's headed for the top of the ladder, not for trouble."

Sandy thought on that for another long minute before answering.

"Perhaps," he allowed, "but let the man tell you himself."

Abruptly, he strode out of the dingy little office and returned a few minutes later with Louis Koch.

"Koch," he said, not unkindly, "tell the boss what you told me this morning."

Louis looked at Mr. Kendall and then looked at the floor.

"I'm going to quit, Mr. Kendall," he said in a low tone.

"Quit!" exclaimed Mr. Kendall. "Why, son, you've got a whole future here ahead of you! You've made a tremendous start! Why, in Heaven's name, do you want to quit?"

Louis looked at Mr. Kendall again and then looked away.

"Fact is, Mr. Kendall," he said, still in a low tone, "I don't like it here."

Mr. Kendall stared in disbelief.

"You don't *like* it here? Why, son, what is there *not* to like? You're making top pay, chances for promotion are good—what more should a man want?" Then, as a sudden thought occurred to him, "Do you want to go back to the farm? Is that it?"

Louis looked unhappy.

"I'm sorry to be so much trouble, Mr. Kendall. I really am. The pay here is real nice. I never made so much money in my whole life."

Then he raised his head and looked Mr. Kendall in the eye.

"The other fellows in the shop don't like me, Mr. Kendall. I don't know why, but they don't. I see them in the shop looking at me. They look at me all during lunch, too. They talk about me, but they don't say anything to me. The fact is, Mr. Kendall," he continued quietly, "the fact is, they hate me."

The three men were silent now. Outside the foreman's office the machines screeched and moaned. Mr. Kendall had slumped back into Sandy's grimy old swivel chair. It was all clear now, too clear. If he had thought it through, he wouldn't have had to ask.

*   *   *

In telling the story of Louis Koch, we have tried to paint a word picture of what happens in an organization when someone defies the group. Louis is a "rate-breaker"—someone who produces more than the other workers think he should. And because he has defied the group, he is suffering the consequences: hostility, rejection, and the feeling of helplessness and anxiety that results.

Because anxiety is so potent, and because it is so painful, few employees become rate-breakers. Most workers are not even aware that they are limiting their production in order to conform to group norms and thus avoid anxiety. Louis is an exception largely because he did not know any better, or, at least, did not understand the customs of the shop. If he had grown up in an industrial environment, he would have understood better what was happening. Then, at least, if he had decided to increase his production above the norm, he would have known that he would arouse resentment and suspicion and he would have been prepared for it. But since he comes from the farm, where individual initiative is valued more highly, he does not see that his unusually high production threatens the psychological security of his fellow workers. But he *does* understand that they hate him. Since he cannot stand and fight a whole group, he has decided to go away. No one likes to feel lost and helpless, and Louis is no exception.

Perhaps another man in Louis' position would not have gone away, but would have stuck it out. Very often such people become the foremen and supervisors of industry. Other persons would have ferreted out the fact that the rest of the workers felt that they were overproducing and would have voluntarily cut their production rather than incur the continued hostility of the group. The important thing is that we feel that we have to *do something* about hostility—fight it, run away from it, or give in to it. When we are rejected and excluded from the group, we cannot easily stand the pain of the anxiety that results, with its feeling of being abandoned and helpless, for very long periods.

*   *   *

What we have been talking about for the most part in this chapter is the anxiety that develops when groups express hostility toward individuals, or when individuals are afraid that groups *might* become hostile. We might call this group-to-person hostility. this is kind of hostility that Howard Galvin encountered in the Every-Member-Canvass Committee meeting.

But there is also the kind of hostility that develops between individuals, what we might call person-to-person hostility.

There are a variety of reasons why person-to-person hostility produces anxiety. For one thing, the expression of *any* kind of hostility is likely to remind us of times when we have been subjected to rejection and disapproval by people whose good opinion is important to us.

However, there is another important reason why hostility of this sort makes us anxious. It is a normal and natural reaction for us to want to strike back and retaliate when others insult, offend, or frustrate us. When someone shoves a preschool child, he shoves him back. One nine-year-old calls another an obscenity, and the other child yells something back or starts to roughhouse with him. These are direct acts of aggression, touched off by the hostile behavior of others.

But as we mature and grow to adulthood, the number of occasions that allow for direct retaliation become fewer and fewer. Few societies tolerate unrestrained expression of interpersonal hostility. Furthermore, most of us are aware that repaying hostility with hostility is futile. No one knows this better than the effective leader. Take Mr. Kendall in the last anecdote. When it dawned on him that the employees in the generator shop were not only limiting their production but were making life miserable for the only man in the shop producing up to capacity, probably nothing would have given him greater pleasure than to go out and fire the whole crew. Yet he knows that he cannot engage in such reckless acts and maintain the plant as a producing unit at the same time. Therefore, he must contain his rage, find some other outlet, or act as though he weren't angry—at least he must behave this way when he talks to the men in the shop. If he is to operate successfully, he must continue to look for ways to get workers to produce more efficiently and effectively. But he knows that to lose his temper (or, at least, to lose it too often) is to lose the battle.

Howard Galvin, in a way, would like to tell Ed off. He would like to tell him that he is tired of having him act like a prima donna and that it is time for him to settle down and stop being so childish. Yet he is aware that such behavior would not be wise, and that the best thing is to handle Ed with kid gloves, although he still has not been able to figure out what he can do beyond this to deal with Ed successfully.

Howard would also like to tell the steno pool what he thinks of office help who take 45-minute coffee breaks. He would like to tell Ollie that she is not being honest when she implies that the other work will suffer if she is required to give him his report when he expects it. But instead of expressing his hostility freely, he maintains a firm grip on himself and says what needs to be said.

Keeping a firm grip on oneself when one is irritated or frightened or angry very often produces anxiety. This is particularly true when we are uncertain what we should do next. Almost any of us will get anxious when we have to control our own hostility. The more effective we are as leaders, the less trouble we will have with this problem. People who are effective leaders can accept and tolerate hostility directed at them because they know how to behave under such conditions. They know that the important thing is not to let the hostility of one or two persons upset the group or interfere with the program of the organization, although it is often desirable to recognize and accept such hostility, since it shows the membership of the group, among other things, that the leader believes that people have a right to be irritated at times and to express this irritation. The point is that the effective leader is more concerned about the welfare of the group than he is about how he feels personally. Less effective leaders either get too upset by attacks made by individual members and go out of their way to defend themselves and their program or else they go too far in pretending that the hostility isn't there.

Persons who have not learned how to handle the hostility expressed by others are likely to be more or less troubled by anxiety, because they feel helpless to cope with the situation. Howard Galvin is anxious about Ed and about the Every-Member-Canvass Committee; his vague feeling of helplessness is both a cause and a result of his anxiety. However, because he has the makings of an effective leader, his morale is good. He feels that eventually he will work out a way to deal with these problems. He also has some confidence in the people with whom he works. He knows that, basically, Ed and Ollie, as well as the Committee members, *want* to be effective members of the organization even though something seems to be interfering at present with the expression of this desire. He also knows that with time, patience, and study he will be able to change his own behavior and eliminate some of the factors that interfere with the effectiveness and cooperation of the people with whom he works. It is too much to expect that he eliminate all such factors. This is partly because few, if any, of us are able to attain the ideal standards we have set for ourselves, but also because much of the hostility that leader must face comes from sources that are beyond their reach.

CHAPTER THREE

Origins of Hostility

In order to identify and analyze the hostility that authority figures unwittingly generate, we shall in this chapter attempt to view them from the standpoint of subordinates—those who are managed, supervised, directed, taught, led, or otherwise influenced. The viewpoint we shall assume is familiar to all—even to authority figures. Anyone who occupies a position of leadership or authority must at times be influenced by others possessing greater power or expertise. In any event, even the most prestigious authority figure must at times play subordinate roles. The president of the republic becomes a patient, when examined by a physician; constitutional monarchs must accept the direction of their prime ministers in political matters; and even prime ministers must (or should) follow the advice of their accountants in ordering their finances.

The basic problem that causes us to feel hostile toward leaders and other figures stems from our mixed emotions or ambivalence about wanting to enjoy the benefits of membership in social groups and at the same time resenting the price that such membership entails. At times, we wish we could get along without belonging to the larger group that is society or the smaller groups that compose it, because belonging to such groups means that our freedom of thought and action will be more or less restricted. But, on the other hand, there are so many advantages in being participating members. For instance, there is the opportunity to meet our normal needs for affection, acceptance, fellowship, and friendship. Without these, life would be empty indeed. Therefore we must surrender some of our freedoms, willingly or not. Some of us enter into the bargain eagerly, because the rewards are so attractive; others of us do so only begrudgingly, deciding only reluctantly that the compromise is unavoidable. Still others hope that the rewards of being accepted by other persons will not require them to conform or adjust their lives in accordance with the demands of society. They continue to hope, unrealistically and neurotically, that they can avoid the responsibilities and requirements that are a part of being a member of society.

We all have, on occasion, attempted to take somewhat more than our reasonable share of society's rewards and have been rebuffed. At other times we have felt cheated or exploited because we have not received what we considered to have been our fair share. Inasmuch as we are human, and hence fallible, we normally believe that the second type of outcome is experienced by us far more frequently that the first type. Irrespective of whether we feel our treatment by others has been justified or not, we are inclined to feel resentful—that is, hostile. But only in unusual instances do we turn our backs on society and withdraw. The more usual practice is to accept setbacks philosophically or begrudgingly and go on with the business of living.

We may feel like expressing some of our hostility toward the group in which we hold membership—society, the community, the organization, or whatever—for having frustrated us, let us down, or condoned our exploitation. But the group is a difficult target. It is hard to focus on the group and harder still to tell the group—particularly a large group—how one feels. There is nothing ambiguous about the individuals who represent the group—persons in positions of authority. Very often it is they who must carry out the policies and regulations of the group and enforce conformity. Thus the person who is ruled out of order by the presiding officer may feel that the latter "has it in for me," the person who is arrested for speeding may feel bitter toward the arresting policeman (rather than toward society), and the person who is fired for off-the-job misconduct may accuse his employer of being intolerant. In the latter instance, the employee may feel that what he does off the job is his own business. He does not see that the employer is expressing the general attitude of society, or, if he does see him in that light, he resents his employer's taking on the role of protector of public morals.

*   *   *

Another source of hostility, and one which is related to our mixed feelings about the group, is our conflict about being dependent on authority figures.

Here, again, is our desire to feel that we are capable of acting independently, of handling our own affairs without help from anyone. In some ways, we resent the fact that we can be helped by another, or that we need to have someone tell us what to think or what to do. It is disconcerting to think that we have lived all the years of our lives and still cannot think and act for ourselves. This is one reason why some people do not go to doctors until it is too late—they cannot accept the thought of having to turn even to an expert for advice. The fact that the doctor is more expert than they in matters of health is beside the point; they are more concerned about the anxiety they would feel if they had to admit that they needed help, that they were, in certain respects, helpless. Many people will not become involved in any transaction which requires them to borrow or even owe money for a short time. For them, being in debt carries the stigma of weakness. Still other persons are unteachable—they cannot admit that someone knows more than they or that they need to learn anything.

Part of this conflict goes back to childhood and adolescence, when we were in the process of becoming independent of our parents. When we were children, we longed for the freedom that adults seemed to have. During adolescence, when we were as large as adults and obviously knew as much or more than they did, we sometimes had the feeling of having to fight for every bit of freedom we received. And it is very likely that our parents *did* make more decisions for us than was necessary. It is hard for parents to let go the reins of authority. In this respect they are like most leaders. In any event, we resented our parents' interference with our freedom, and we vowed to ourselves that when *we* got to be adults, no one would put us back into bondage.

As adults, most of us realize that we are not as free as we thought we would be when we were children. Most of the time we can accept the restrictions and responsibilities as part of being an adult in a complex, modern society. But there are times when persons in authority remind us of the days when we were engaged in a struggle for freedom with our parents, and it seems to us that persons in authority are demanding too much, are expecting too much, or are, as we say, "getting too big for their jobs." And at such times we are strongly moved to express our hostility in the way that is most appropriate both to the situation and to the kind of person we are.

But there is another side to this matter of being independent. There is pretty good evidence that each of us secretly (or unconsciously) longs to be dependent, and that much of our struggle to be independent is part of a maneuver to keep ourselves from realizing how deep our needs for dependency really are. This means that in some ways we actually *like* being dependent. We like to have authority figures show us special favors, we like to have them tell us that they like us, we like to be promoted to positions "closer to the throne." And on those occasions when a leader favors someone else or fails to notice our honest efforts, life can look very dark.

Because our needs for dependency are hidden even from our own eyes, we are likely to feel rather guilty about them. Since we like to think of ourselves as independent, self-sufficient individuals, we rather resent even our own needs for dependency. Hence, at those times when we get twinges of wanting to be dependent on leaders, of wanting favors from them, or of wanting them to decide something for us, we push such feelings from our consciousness and make a show of resentment toward the leaders in question, as though *they* were to blame for our desire for attention. Implicit in some of our resentment about leaders who are particularly dominating is the feeling that we don't want to be "treated like a child." One of the reasons why it is so annoying to be treated like a child is that at times, and to some degree (unconsciously, that is), we would like to get rid of our adult responsibilities at one stroke and be as carefree as children again. On the one hand, we are made anxious when we think of losing the support and favor of the leader, but on the other hand, we resent needing his support and protection. We both want and need his power to help us, but we are also afraid of it and resent it.

*   *   *

Some of these inconsistencies in how we feel are the result of an unrealistic or neurotic outlook on life, but some of them are also the result of the unhappy experiences we have had with people who have more power, prestige, and authority than we do.

There was the older child, when we were in elementary school, who demanded a share of our lunch money—for "protection." The consequences of not yielding to his demands were frightening, so we gave in and thus learned about the world and its injustices.

There was the teacher who made us work hard at drawings and paintings that she used to decorate the room. She said that she did this because children enjoy drawing and painting, and besides, the pictures made the room look so pretty. But she only used the ones that she liked and threw the rest away. A few children were more artistic than others, and they were the only ones whose pictures were displayed. So, after a while, we realized that she did this to impress the principal, the other teachers, and the parents. She really didn't mean what she said about giving children opportunities to do something they enjoyed.

There was the IRS agent who exacted a penalty when we could not find a cancelled check to back up a charitable donation we definitely had made. And the fact that we had to take a half-day's annual leave for the tax audit made us feel doubly resentful.

We could go on and on—any of us—and recount similar incidents to show that persons in authority *have* taken advantage of us countless numbers of times. Of course, if we try, we can also think of many more times when leaders helped us and when it was very good just to have a leader in charge. The point is, because we have all had experiences in which leaders took advantage of their position, we feel that we should be on guard against this happening again, just as we feel, because of our experiences when leaders and persons in authority limited our freedom more than was necessary or just, that we must be on constant guard against further infringement of our rights and liberties.

Thus the unfortunate experiences we have had with leaders and persons in authority (including our own parents) provide some of the force behind the feelings of hostility that we bear toward the leaders we now have. In a way, we are inclined to punish our present leaders for the sins of former ones. Or, rather, we are inclined to lump leaders and persons in authority into one group and behave toward them as though they were all alike. So we say, "Policemen are like that," or "Isn't that just the way with teachers?" or "I never saw a boss that wouldn't take advantage of you." Or, more likely, we say nothing at all, but are on our guard, on the defensive, against *all* leaders, *all* persons in authority with whom we must deal.

Such an attitude of being continually on the defensive is the seedbed of hostility; it is from such beginnings that the many manifestations of hostility develop.

Hostility, like other forms of human behavior, does not result from a single event or condition; it is the product of many forces and experiences combined. Thus the hostility of a given employee or group member is very likely the result of all or most of the factors we have described, assuming that we have, for the most part, mentioned problems and conditions that are common to most of us and that are a part of our everyday environment.

*   *   *

However, there is another factor that is also rather crucial, one that is in the background, overshadowing much of the relationship between leader and group member, between supervisor and subordinate: *hostility toward leaders is part of our cultural heritage.* Indeed, one might say that we have a kind of tradition about being hostile toward those who supervise and guide our activities.

America was settled by people who objected to the established order of things in their homeland. They were people who resisted and resented having their minds made up for them by persons in authority. Some came to America to be free to worship as they saw fit; others came because they longed for the freer, more "natural" life of the wilderness. By seeking freedom, they were thereby rejecting and avoiding coercion and conformity.

The civilization that developed on our Atlantic seaboard was in some respects freer and in some respects more restrictive than that of Mother Europe. Probably the net effect was one of greater freedom for the individual. But even this relative freedom was not enough for the new crop of rugged individualists who grew up in succeeding generations. As they found the bonds of civilization too restraining, they, too, went westward into the wilderness to escape from conformity and to search for freedom. Somehow, they found it easier to accept the impersonal dictates of the forces of nature than the more personalized restrictions and limitations that come with living in close proximity to others. And so the country was settled, with the rebels against authority and conformity in each generation seeking freedom farther to the West, with their numbers supplemented by new waves of immigrants in search of political, economic, religious, and intellectual, personal freedom.

Although the frontier vanished toward the end of the 19th century, its traditions have a strong influence on our thoughts and attitudes today.

Perhaps it is nowhere more pronounced than in the fervent desire of individual Americans to be free and independent and in their wariness lest any person or organization get too much power. This attitude, for example, is expressed in our structure of laws, such as the limitation on the power and freedom of the President and the Congress, the legislation against monopolies, and the laws limiting the power and freedom of both management and labor. It is true that these laws have been developed to meet specific political and economic needs, but their philosophy has generally been guided by the principle of not permitting concentrations of power that might interfere with the basic freedom and rights of individuals.

As a result, Americans are inclined to be more than usually suspicious of persons in positions of authority as compared to persons from other cultures. We are more outspoken and, according to the standards of the citizens of other lands, are more "disrespectful" toward our leaders.

Some of our hostility toward leaders stems from a strong feeling that every individual is equal to every other individual, that no one should represent himself as being better. This feeling shows up in such different phases of our national life as the "soak-the-rich" tax movement during the Depression of the 1930's, the bitterness that was prevalent among enlisted men during World War II regarding the special privileges enjoyed by officers,and our well-known partiality for the underdog.

Sometimes our hostile feelings about the privileges of rank and status come into conflict with other needs. On the one hand, we want the Mayor to have a brand new Cadillac. Being a mayor is an important job. He represents all of us, the whole city, and it is only right that such an important man, holding an important office, elected by the citizens of an important community should have a large and important automobile. So we get him a Cadillac.

The next year we think: "Who does the Mayor think he is anyway? *We* have to get along with Fords and Chevrolets. Does he think he is better than we are? Let him get along with a Ford like the rest of us." On the one hand, we want to build up the status of our leaders because we admire them, but, on the other hand, we want to tear them down to our size, lest they get any "big ideas."

And tear them down we do. Leaders in a democratic society are more vulnerable, more open to attack than are leaders in autocratic, authoritarian societies. A leader in a democratic society does have more power than the persons he supervises or leads, but he must be exceedingly careful of how he uses his power, particularly when he uses it to attack someone of lesser power and importance. It is traditional in this country that any citizen can criticize any person of power and importance without running the risk of severe reprisals, and when the public is alerted to instances of persons in authority using their greater power to avenge themselves on some critic, the expression of popular disapproval has often resulted in the removal or the silencing of the offending official.

Because Americans have less reason to be afraid of retaliation on the part of leaders, they are probably more likely to attack them. Thus, criticizing government or management or any set of leaders is a favorite pastime. Indeed, there is some evidence that such complaints may be a very healthy kind of activity. One study of the behavior of workers showed that chronic gripers were among the most efficient producers.

Because of our resentment of superior airs on the part of leaders, many of them lean over backward to avoid anything that may smack of aristocratic leanings. Political candidates make a show of being photographed at simple chores like milking or riveting, and captains of industry sometimes make quite a point of being called by their first names. Although much of this is obviously for show, undoubtedly much of it is motivated by a desire to be genuinely democratic and not to lose contact with the lives of the people these individuals lead or employ.

*   *   *

By now it should be clear that our hostility towards leaders has many causes. It stems from our conflicting feelings about groups and about society in general, about being independent of leaders and dependent on them at the same time, about our relations with our parents, about being free of the entangling restrictions of "civilization," and about whether we want leaders to be "better" than the rest of us. Since these feelings are with us most of the time, to a greater or lesser degree, it is easy to see how a leader might become the innocent target for a great deal of unearned hostility, and how the very presence of a person of authority and position can arouse tensions among his subordinates. Even to be near a person who has much power and authority over us usually arouses some anxiety. The more power he has over our everyday life, the more he stimulates the conflicts we have regarding leaders, the more anxious we become. This anxiety does not immediately give rise to hostility. That usually comes later.

The next day, after we think about our experiences in talking to the boss or the senator or the general or the doctor—whoever this person of authority was—we may resent the feeling of helplessness that he was able to arouse in us, as well as the fact that someone could be so superior to us in power. And perhaps we sense what dangerous people leaders are—after all, they can make us do things that we may not want to do. And we begin to wonder whether we really want to do the things that they think we should do. Some of us react to this sequence of events by refusing to do what is expected of us, or by finding reasons not to do it. Somehow we didn't get the job done the way the boss wanted it, or we told ourselves that generals are all "stuffed shirts," or we forgot to take the medicine the doctor had prescribed. Even when we were asked to do things in our own best interests, we let our irritation at being made to feel helpless interfere to the point that it becomes more important to retaliate than to do what was expected.

What we have described in the above paragraph is, of course, only one broad pattern of hostile reaction. Another kind of person may feel equally hostile but may turn his hostility upon himself. He may feel so guilty about having feelings of resentment toward the person of authority that he actually outdoes himself in trying to do what was expected of him.

May Bauman is this kind of person. She was at the top of her class when she took shorthand and typing at business college. She rather enjoyed shorthand and used to take down radio broadcasts now and then, just for the practice. But when she graduated and took a job at the Herold Corporation, things were different. Shorthand wasn't any fun any more. It was quite different when you had to sit across the desk from Mr. Minor or any of the other men in the office and try to get their ideas down on paper. Mr. Minor mumbled and kept going back over what he had said and changing things, but that wasn't what made May feel uncomfortable. Come to think of it, she couldn't say for sure *what* it was that she didn't like about taking dictation. Maybe it was the idea that what Mr. Minor and the other supervisors were saying was pretty important, that she had to get it right or it would cost the company money. It wasn't that they were so particular or anything like that, but just the same after May had been taking dictation for an hour steady, she was just as tense and jittery as if she had been on a roller-coaster. It took the whole afternoon for her to get it out of her system.

When she came back to her desk after a long siege of dictation, she would try to start in as though nothing had happened, but almost invariably, she would make a mistake before she had got halfway through the first letter. So she'd rip the letter out of the machine and start over again. Sometimes it would take four starts on a letter before she'd get control of herself again.

She always worked much harder at dictation and transcription than she did at anything else in her work. Mr. Minor and some of the other men even praised the neatness and accuracy of her work, but May never got any real pleasure from their compliments. In a way, she was afraid that if she said anything favorable they would get the idea that she *liked* dictation. She envied the others who did straight typing and even thought of asking to be transferred to that kind of work, but the thought of taking a cut in salary gave her pause. Besides, how would she explain her demotion to her family and to the rest of the people in the office?

The thing that really got under May's skin is that her attitude was actually very silly. After all, she *was* an expert stenographer, and there was *no real reason* why she should be nervous about a little dictation. Sometimes at night, after a particularly bad day at the office, she would lie awake and try to figure out why she was so disturbed at taking letters. She was never able to figure out any reasons. And so she would scold and lecture herself:

"What a silly goose you are, May Bauman, to be afraid of a simple thing like taking dictation. Mr. Minor, Mr. Shubert, and the other supervisors aren't going to bite your head off if you turn out a letter with a mistake in it. Besides, your letters almost never have any mistakes. When was the last one? Weeks ago. You can't even remember when it was. It's silly to be nervous. Now tomorrow, when Mr. Minor calls you into his offfice, you walk in, look him in the eye, sit down and go to work. No nerves. No reason for it...."

And of course, the next day, she would be just as nervous as ever. After each session, she would be angry with herself for having been so silly and for having been unable to suppress her feeling of anxiety. Thank goodness, she was able to keep from showing it ... Or *was* she? Well, at any rate, the safest thing to do was to turn out perfect work and get everything done on time or ahead of time. Then, surely, no one would be able to criticize her.

Every so often, May would wish that Mr. Minor and the other supervisors wouldn't put so much pressure on her. There were, for example, the times when they were giving her dictation so often that she could barely catch her breath between taking dictation and transcription. At such times, it seemed to her that they regarded her as some kind of dictating machine, something that they could just dictate to and a letter would come out automatically. Or she would complain to some of the other girls. But always, afterward, she would feel guilty and would go to extra pains to see that her letters were above reproach....

*   *   *

Probably the bulk of the routine paperwork of the world is accomplished by people like May Bauman, people who have learned to turn their hostility toward themselves and to express it through working harder, more accurately, and more efficiently. Most of them are not as nervous as May is, but, like her, they are seldom aware of hostile feelings. Their hostility seldom, if ever, arises to the level of personal awareness, but instead seeks expression as perfectionism or as self-criticism. When their anxiety and repressed hostility is especially high, as it is with May, they derive no great pleasure from turning out a perfect piece of work. Their chief reward, rather, is a sense of relief at not having made any errors.

Most of us in today's world use this psychological device to some extent. Turning our hostility toward ourselves has the advantage of keeping our relations with other people, particularly people who are important to us, on a fairly even keel and at the same time releasing energy for constructive work. However, if we are inclined to overwork this approach, we run the risk of stifling creativeness, of becoming afraid of *any* expression of an emotional nature, and of reducing life to a dead-level kind of routine.

CHAPTER FOUR

The Many Masks of Hostility

In the last chapter we explored some of the sources of the hostility which subordinates and group members develop as a result of their relations with supervisors and leaders and we ended with a discussion of one kind of hostility—the kind developed by the "self-punishing person."

Actually, of course, there are a wide variety of ways in which hostility may be expressed, some of them socially acceptable, like the self-critical perfectionism of May Bauman, and some of them less acceptable, like rioting and sabotage. Perhaps it will help our discussion if we examine these various forms of hostile expression under three headings: active, passive, and indirect. There are, of course, no sharp distinctions or differences among these groupings. Nevertheless, these three patterns of hostility do possess definable qualities which will help us to recognize and understand them better when we encounter them among our subordinates and fellow group members.

*   *   *

Let us consider the active forms of hostility first. Not only are they the types that are most readily identified as hostile, but they are also the kinds that arouse the greatest fear and anxiety. Under this heading are included the direct physical expression of hostility, such as assault and battery, sabotage, armed rebellion, rioting, and looting; direct verbal expression, such as cursing, arguing, public expression of disagreement, criticism, written and oral attack, denial, rejection, censure, and certain kinds of political advertising; and various forms of group expression that are neither verbal nor physical, such as strikes, slowdowns, boycotts, and some forms of political action.

There is no question but that the physical expression of hostility interferes with the effectiveness of any group enterprise that is concerned with the positive goals of society. We have real reasons to fear hostility in this form, and the existence of legal codes, courts, prisons, police, and the militia is the visible evidence of our concern.

To a more limited extent, we also have reason to fear the *verbal* expression of hostility. Very often it precedes the more physical forms of hostility. This is particularly true among children and adolescents, as well as among adults who are emotionally immature, relatively uneducated, or who belong to cultures that encourage and permit fist fights, knifings, dueling, feuding, or other physical forms of expressing hostility. However, as far as most of the educated and civilized Western World is concerned, the verbal expression of hostility rarely leads to physical expression. Therefore, we must find other reasons why verbal hostility upsets us so.

One obvious reason is that hostile remarks or statements interfere with the smooth functioning of groups, particularly when these remarks are directed at other members of the group, and most especially when they are directed at the leader. In a way, the amount of hostile interchange is a measure of the extent to which the group is cohesive, the extent to which it is "together" with regard to common objectives. Groups which are not "together," which continually work at cross purposes, and which spend their time in squabbling and disagreement cannot function adequately and efficiently. Therefore it is with some realism that we become anxious when we hear hostile comments. This anxiety is expressed by such well-worn sayings as: "If you can't boost, don't knock," "Let's put our shoulders to the wheel," and "If we don't hang together, we'll hang separately."

But there are other, more obscure reasons why hostile statements cause us to be anxious.

For one thing, they remind us of our own childhood and youth, when physical aggression and punishment were associated with verbal forms of hostility—for example, the physical punishment that sometimes accompanied being scolded or reprimanded, or the fist fights or hair-pullings that were the direct result of childish arguments.

For another, they also recall the emotions that resulted from or accompanied an exchange of verbal hostilities. Angry words meant that someone would be rejected, someone was disapproving of someone else, someone was thought to be inferior, inadequate, and unworthy. It does not matter whether we are the direct target for this hostile expression. We have all had the experience of being in the same room with a friend or a fellow worker or a child who is being reprimanded or scolded. This is an uncomfortable experience, even though the individual concerned may be at fault. We ourselves may not be personally involved, and this may be obvious to everyone. Yet we wonder in a vague sort of way whether if by chance we were really guilty of something or other. Perhaps we are "identifying" with the guilty party, perhaps we feel that the person in authority is being too harsh. Perhaps we wonder whether he would be as harsh with us if *we* were at fault. Or perhaps this is a harkening back to the earliest days of our infancy, when we were made anxious by *any* tension or unhappiness on the part of our mothers, regardless of whether or not it directly applied to us. Very likely *all* of these factors are involved in a more or less simultaneous fashion.

What we have just been saying is that we are made anxious by the hostile statements of others because we are afraid of being attacked or rejected by others, directly or indirectly, or of being excluded from the company of people who are important to us. However, there is another reason for our anxiety, a reason that is, in effect, the mirror image of the reason we have just given—that is, we are also anxious because we are afraid of our own hostility.

Essentially, we are afraid of our own hostility because it has got us into trouble in the past. In other words, we see our own hostility as a contributing cause of hostility in others. Because we "talked back" to our parents, they punished us; because we threw rocks at the boy next door, he knocked us down; because we lost our temper and told the teacher what we thought of him, we got a low grade in the course, and so on. Furthermore, when others start talking in a hostile way, this may lead us to make hostile remarks, and this, in turn, may lead them to attack or to reject us. And so we come to feel that the safest thing is for no one to say anything that smacks of hostility, unless it is about something that is commonly accepted by the group as a suitable target—such as high taxes, the behavior of nonbelievers, sin and corruption, or anything that group members tacitly or openly agree that they are against.

There is another dimension to the anxiety aroused by the expression of hostility, and that is the general feeling of anxious concern that is so typical of the middle-class Western World regarding anything emotional—anything, that is, but the mildest form of emotion. It is much safer, we feel, for relations with others to be maintained on an impersonal basis—let us keep things, as far as possible, on a rational, nonemotional level. We have come to believe that human relations should rest on a basis that is reasonable and logical. If people must display feelings, we say, let these be only *positive* feelings. But even here we believe in restraint, because if we develop and express *strong* positive feelings towards other persons, we may find ourselves involved in responsibilities that we later may have cause to regret. "No," we counsel ourselves, "it is much safer to be restrained. Less embarrassing, too." Hence, even if we had no other reasons to eliminate or repress hostility, we would be likely to do so on the grounds that it is an emotion.

What we have been trying to do in the foregoing passages is to describe common patterns of behavior and belief regarding hostility and have attempted to refrain from stating what is desirable for good mental health. However, we cannot help noting that perhaps we go too far in our attempts to avoid any expression that smacks of hostility. We shall have more to say about the need for free expression in later chapters, hence we shall not go into the subject further at this point except to say that those organizations that are most effective and efficient in the broadest sense, that have the best morale, and that do the best job of meeting the diverse needs of the individuals who compose them are organizations that are less worried and upset about the possible expression of hostility.

What very often happens is that organizations that are the most concerned and the most anxious about hostility are the ones that succeed only in driving it underground, with the result that it expresses itself in less obvious but more destructive ways. And we should point out that one of the dangers in de-emotionalizing or "de-humanizing" human relations is that reason and logic do not constitute an adequate defense against such dangers as poor morale, inefficiency, and dissension. Human beings often develop perverse and distorted patterns of behavior based on what appears to them to be rational and logical grounds. This often leads to the very kind of highly emotionalized situation that they were hoping to avoid through the use of reason and logic. Observe the frustration of the person whose wholly logical solution to a problem is attacked by his friends as being illogical!

The third form of direct hostile expression we mentioned at the beginning of this discussion consisted of group action that could not be classified as verbal or physical—strikes, slowdowns, boycotts, and various forms of political action.

In some respects, these forms of hostility are somewhat passive, in that they very often involve *not* doing something rather than carrying out some directly injurious act. Yet the intent to damage or embarrass someone is obvious to everyone concerned—these are acts of deliberate and conscious defiance; hence we have included them under the heading of direct hostile expression.

This type of hostility differs from the two other types in that it is more deliberate, whereas the direct forms of physical and verbal expression are more likely to be spontaneous. Strikes, slowdowns, and the other forms of hostile behavior in this category always involve concerted group action, whereas the more direct forms of hostility may or may not involve group action. For this reason the problems they pose are of a different nature. For example, a skilled leader can permit a group to "blow off steam" by giving them a chance to express their complaints freely, but dealing with a strike or boycott is quite a different matter.

A strike, for example, usually has a long history. It is the result of a combination of factors, such as a long series of real or fancied grievances, a real feeling of being unable to communicate with persons in power, and the ability of a group to organize themselves for concerted action. Many strikes, too, have a "public relations angle" in that there is an attempt to involve the public somehow, sympathetically or otherwise. A strike serves as an excuse for both workers and management to tell the story of their grievances to the general public. To be sure, both sides run the risk of irritating the public and thus incurring some hostility, but this is often counterbalanced by the opportunity to remind the public of the importance of the services that are now suspended because of the strike. For example, the public tends to take the functions of subway employees and garbage collectors for granted and assigns them relatively low positions in the hierarchy of social status. However, when the public is forced to do without these services, it realizes how important and how essential these workers are. The respect that we, the public, accord them is tinged with impatience and irritation, to be sure, but it seems to be consistent with human nature to prefer negative recognition to no recognition at all. Indeed, the desire for recognition and status, which, after all, is common to everyone, appears to underlie many forms of hostile expression.

*   *   *

Although the active forms of hostility arouse the most acute anxiety and counter-hostility, the passive forms are the most destructive in the long run. Under this heading come such familiar forms of behavior as apathy, boredom, absenteeism, spoilage, and what might be termed the "general inability to understand."

It is annoying and irritating to have to deal with an actively hostile person. You are trying to tell him to do something, and he is telling you that he doesn't like you. But, after all, you and he *are* on a communicative plane—you are still talking to each other. And very likely if you will accept some of his hostility or find some way of diverting it and thus getting it out of the way, it will be possible for the two of you to get on with your business.

But the *passively* hostile person presents quite a different problem. In the first place, he will deny or be unaware that he is hostile at all. He is just "not interested" or "doesn't understand." Or he is tired. He doesn't want to be bothered. Incidentally, one of the ways that expert leaders sometimes use in dealing with such apathy is to nag or bait group members and get them to develop *active* hostility, whereupon they deal with the direct expression of the active hostility. Indeed, it is virtually a truism that passive hostility must be converted into active hostility (of the verbal variety, of course) if it is to be dealt with at all. This conversion doesn't always work, of course. Very often the roots of passive hostility are so deep that a complete change of emotional climate is needed, accompanied by a carefully planned series of situations calculated to draw the individual or group out of the shell of passive hostility.

The individual who is actively hostile is one who feels that he has a chance to *do something* about an unpleasant or undesirable situation. He feels that if he attacks or criticizes or argues or organizes, he may be able to bring about an improvement. This is one of the reasons it is possible to cope with him. He has some hope that his efforts will be rewarded, else he would not have undertaken his hostile acts.

But the individual who is passively hostile is a person who is discouraged. He has given up. He sees no chance that things will get better. He will do those things that he is forced to do, but he sees no percentage in doing them well. He is no longer interested in rewards, he is only concerned with avoiding punishment, discomfort, and anxiety. There is no real communication with a passively hostile individual, because he has a fixed idea that listening for the purpose of understanding is futile.

Harrison Gilmartin looked up from his desk in the corner of the brilliantly lighted relay assembly room as George Hill, his immediate supervisor, came around the corner. He sighed as he got to his feet. That preoccupied look on George's face foreshadowed trouble. And when he saw the teletype in George's hand, he *knew* there would be trouble.

George dropped down on an empty chair and motioned for Harrison to sit down.

"Thought you'd like to be the first to know," he grinned, holding up the teletype. "Latest word; hot off the wires."

Harrison reached for it and said, without looking to see what it read:

"George, if it's another basic change in our X-34 relay, I'll resign. So help me, I don't want to live through another change-over like that."

George flashed another grin.

"Oh, relax," he said. "This one's easy. You could do this one in your sleep. Go on, read it; see what it says."

Harrison read the wire through and then read it again, mentally rearranging the parts of the relay, weighing what was involved in this latest change. When he was through, he leaned back and looked at George.

"Well," he admitted, "it's not a major change, but mark my words, it'll be no picnic."

George was serious now, and he looked at Harrison intently.

"What gives, Harrison?" he asked. "Why is it that any kind of change throws your department for a loop? Your daily production reports show that your gang still haven't made up the production they lost when we changed over to the new design three weeks ago."

Harrison made a gesture of exasperation.

"Damn it, George," he exclaimed, "you know me well enough to know that I'd like to have the answer to that one, too. There's not a reason in the world why they should have lost any more than a week's production on that last changeover. The number of parts is the same; the number of motions is the same. But I can't seem to get them off the dime. I've talked to them, threatened them, but they all tell me the same thing: the new relay is a lot more difficult than the old one. Now you and I both know that's a lot of hogwash. I've seen the reports from Middlefield, where they're making the same relay, and they were back to normal in a week. I even fired a couple of women who had been dragging their feet more than the others and whose absentee record was pretty bad. The production at their tables actually went up for a couple of days after that, but it dropped back down again."

He paused for a minute, picked up a paper clip and started to bend it into a triangle. Then he put it down and looked steadily at George.

"I guess you know that this situation has really been getting under my skin," he said. "A couple of weeks ago I began to wonder what was wrong with *me*. I was pretty sure it wasn't the women. I have fifty of them, all sizes, shapes, and colors, just like the women employed in the other parts of the plant. They do O.K. when they work for Morse or Hargreaves or Murray. But they don't do O.K. when they work for me. I felt pretty low when I thought that out. And then I thought, "Who in heaven's name ever said you were a supervisor anyhow? You're an engineer, and a damn good engineer, too. You've got no business sitting behind a desk, breaking your heart just because you can't knock some sense into the heads of a few dozen silly women.' "

"No, George," he concluded, "this isn't for me. I'm requesting a transfer to the research lab. It'll cost me $3000 a year in salary, but it'll be worth it."

One of the things that Harrison is trying to cope with is, of course, passive hostility. He is dealing with a group of workers who resent changes in their work situation over which they have no control. Undoubtedly, they would accept them if they understood why the changes had to be made, but Harrison has not thought to make such explanation to them, and from the description we have of their present attitude, it would seem that such an attempt would be coming too late, for they would no longer be interested in listening. That is, they might go through the motions of listening, but their hearts would not be in it, they would not listen with the will to learn and understand. Hence, at this point, little of value would be gained.

Harrison is more perceptive than many supervisors, however. He realizes that he does not have the skills or the interests to bring about the necessary changes in the situation, and he is willing to defer to someone who is more skilled in human relations than he. Just the same, he cannot resist expressing some exasperation over the inability of his employees to "be sensible" about the job at hand. His exasperation is understandable, because there are few things so frustrating as having to deal with passive hostility.

It is far more personally satisfying to deal with the person who expresses his hostility actively. After all, he is "guilty" of something or other—insubordination, rebellion, verbal attack, or whatever. Because he has attacked us in some way, we feel justified in retaliation. He has hurt us, or has tried to hurt us, so we will hurt him back. Perhaps we deal harshly with him but we feel justified—after all, didn't he attempt to injure us?

But the person who expresses his hostility *passively* cannot be punished so easily. He has done *nothing*. There is nothing that we can pick up as an excuse for revenge or retaliation. He is a most unsatisfactory antagonist, because he does not provide us with any opening or any opportunity to get back at him. Yet he blocks us just as successfully, or even more successfully, as the openly hostile person.

*   *   *

There are a great variety of ways of expressing hostility that come under the heading of "indirect." One method is self-punishment, as exemplified by the behavior of May Bauman, described in the last chapter. The more the self-punisher feels the pressure of hostility, the more pressure he puts on himself to conform and to do what is expected of him by persons in authority. And, as we suggested previously, this kind of maneuver often has the effect of stifling originality and spontaneity. Such persons are afraid to do anything out of the ordinary for fear of directing attention to themselves and thus calling forth the disapproval of both superiors and peers.

A rather extreme form of self-punishment is the accident-prone person. In some respects he belongs in the passive-hostility category, too, depending on the extent to which his accidents involve others. Some accident-prone people are responsible for a great deal of breakage and spoilage. Try as they might, they do not seem to avoid having accidents of this sort. Persons of this type are very likely expressing hostility toward the group or toward the persons in authority, hostility of whose existence they are largely unaware. But then there are the persons whose accidents involve only themselves. They, too, are usually unaware of the existence and nature of their hostility. Very often, their accidents seem designed to help them get out of uncomfortable situations, such as the case of the boy who detests school and manages to stay out of it for several months when he happens to break a leg. In most cases, there is no conscious intent to precipitate an accident—it just happens. And it "happens" oftener with some people than with others—hence the term "accident-prone." The vast majority of highway and industrial accidents are caused by a small minority of the population, a minority that becomes involved in accidents repeatedly. For these people, having accidents is a way of avoiding anxiety and expressing hostility. Accidents may have other psychological purposes which are served concurrently—the boy we just mentioned may also enjoy the attention he gets because of his broken leg—but there is almost always some undercurrent of hostility involved.

Competitiveness is also a way of expressing hostility more or less indirectly. We say "more or less," because competitiveness, like accident-proneness, may also appear in direct forms of behavior, and may even be directed against persons in authority. However, competitive persons are usually unaware of what they are doing—that is, that they are engaging in hostile acts. This general unawareness is why we have listed competitiveness under the indirect expression of hostility.

Competitiveness differs from most of the other methods of hostile expression we have covered in that it is socially acceptable. In fact, people are *expected* to compete in our Western culture. Consequently, many a salesman who has been given an assignment that he would otherwise resent, diverts the energy that would be used to express his resentment in rolling up a sales record that is better than those made by the other men in his department. And many a leader has been able to divert hostility, that would normally be expressed toward management, by stirring up competition among his subordinates. Sometimes this competition has had a healthy or useful outcome, in that it served to involve employees in promoting the welfare of the organization. But at other times competition turns out to be a destructive force, an expression of the "divide-and-conquer" principle.

Many students of human relations have raised the question of whether we tend to overvalue the contributions of competition. Unfortunately, of course, many of us are more concerned about competing than we are about cooperating. Indeed, there are some who give the impression that they have never learned how to cooperate and do not care to try.

Still another form of indirect expression of hostility, one that is socially approved, is what psychologists call *sublimation*. This is a maneuver whereby we work off resentment through involving ourselves in some useful or creative or otherwise acceptable activity. Thus the minister who is frustrated and irritated by the failure of the board of trustees to support him on an important issue spends the next day chopping wood for his fireplace and finds that he can face the situation more philosophically. Or the high school principal, after an exceedingly frustrating day trying to sort out students for registration, spends a quiet evening identifying and classifying stamps for his collection—at least *they* will stay where you put them! Or the salesman who has had a trying day pushing his line finds satisfaction in watching wrestling on the television set.

One could go on endlessly listing the various ways in which people "sublimate" their hostility. Some of these outlets for hostility are active, like chopping wood, and some of them are passive, like watching television, but they all have a common factor—they help to relieve the anxiety and hostility that would otherwise build up in the individuals concerned, anxiety and hostility that, if left unexpressed, would interfere with their happiness and general effectiveness. Most usually the process of sublimation goes on unconsciously—that is, the individual automatically or almost instinctively turns to some activity that will help rid himself of his bitterness in a harmless or constructive way. If this attempt is successful, he learns, after a while, to turn to that activity which has effectively relieved his tension.

There are a wide variety of activities that serve dual purposes—that is, they serve as outlets for hostility and at the same time meet the creative needs for individuals. Winston Churchill and many other persons in all walks of life have found oil painting a way of meeting this need. Some people write poetry; some serve as leaders of youth groups. Others engage in amateur dramatics, and still others find creative release through political activities. And many, many others find an opportunity for creativity and a satisfying outlet for their hostility in their everyday work.

What we do is not important, as long as it enables us to employ our talents creatively (in the very broadest sense of that word) and at the same time releases some of the inner pressure of hostility, resentment, and anxiety. The important thing is for individuals to lose themselves for a while in some sort of activity that will permit equilibrium to be restored and will relax the tension induced by anxiety and hostility. If this activity can be creative, so much the better.

One of the tasks of the effective leader is to recognize the need among his subordinates or group members to work off hostility, preferably through creative activity, and to arrange ways whereby this need may be met. He must, of course, be able to do this skillfully, sympathetically, and in a way that will not offend the self-sufficiency of the persons he supervises. It is quite one thing for the president of the company to decide that the employees need a bowling alley, proceed to build one, and direct the heads of departments to organize bowling teams and competitions. It is quite another for a company to help the employees organize a recreation group, help them decide on the kind of facilities they want, and assist them in planning recreational affairs. The end result in both situations may be competitive bowling among departments, but the first method runs the danger of humiliating employees and arousing hostility and apathy, whereas the second gives them the feeling of participation and self-sufficiency,without making them feel that the company is trying to run their lives outside of working hours.

$$*\qquad*\qquad*$$

Under the heading of sublimation, we have mentioned some *positive* ways that we work off hostility and anxiety. There are, of course, many other means of accomplishing the same end that are less attractive from the standpoint of social utility or creativity. They range from the mild to the serious.

Jim Clancy expected to be elected to the post of Grand Secretary when his lodge convened for the annual state-wide meeting, but they elected some guy he never even heard of. He was very bitter about the whole thing that evening after the meeting was over. He didn't even want to go out and have a drink with the fellows from his home lodge, but they talked him into having just one. After a couple of drinks, he wasn't as mad as he was earlier in the evening. An hour or so later, he was even willing to admit that it was probably for the best. And when the new Grand Secretary wandered into the bar toward the end of the evening, Jim discovered that he was one of the nicest guys he had ever met.

Nora Kurz was so mad she couldn't even talk when Miss Ricci, the supervisor, spoke to her about being late so many times. After all, nobody else in the office had to transfer three times on the way to work. She sat down at her desk for a minute and then decided that she'd better have a cigarette. In the restroom she ran into Pat and Ethel who had the desks in front of hers. Her eyes lit up.

"Did you find out who Miss Ricci has been going to lunch with?" she asked.

"Yeah," Pat replied. "It's some kid in the stockroom."

"You'd think she'd pick 'em her own age, wouldn't you?" Nora commented. "But I suppose that when you get to be thirty, I guess you can't afford to be choosey."

"Thirty!" exclaimed Ethel. "Her personnel record says she is twenty-five. Last time I was helping out down in personnel I looked to see."

"Don't let it fool you," Nora said. "My boyfriend's brother is pretty sure that she was in his class in high school, and he graduated *twelve years* ago. That would make her thirty by my count...."

     *   *   *

Ted DuBois had just lost his job. Sure, it was just a job and he could get another easy enough. But what really burned him was the way they did it. When the manager told him that it was because of his difficulties with the other employees, Ted had smelled a rat. He was easily the most popular guy in the office, so he knew there must be something odd somewhere. So he asked who was replacing him. Turned out to be Don Klee. Don Klee, the boss's nephew. How do you like that? No point in talking it over with the wife. She'd just say that the boss was probably right. No, the best thing would be just to wait till after supper, then tell her and leave. But he'd have to have a reason to leave ... Oh sure, the Wednesday night poker game. How could he have forgotten? He never missed the Wednesday night poker game. It was as sacred as the Rock of Ages or something. The only night a week he was sure of getting out....

Ted went to the Wednesday night poker game. He was always a wide-open player, but this time he played it wider and wilder than usual. He didn't drop out of a single pot all evening long. At first he had amazing luck; the cards were with him. But as the evening drew on, the tide turned, and when the game ended at 12:30, as it always did, he was out $200. For a penny a chip and a nickel limit, that's pretty heavy losses....

     *   *   *

As John Lloyd closed up the photography department at Gunsky's that evening, he had every reason to feel good. Within a few minutes he would be sitting down at the monthly dinner meeting of the buyers and department heads, waiting for the announcement of the winners of the monthly sales improvement contest. John had won the first three contests of the year because his sales had showed the greatest percentage-wise increase over last year. He had every expectation of being announced as the winner again tonight, and for the fourth time running! He could practically feel the $100 prize-money check crackling in his pocket.

Later, at the dinner, after the dessert had been cleared away and a haze of cigar and cigarette smoke filled the room, John relaxed over a cup of coffee and waited for the announcement. He did not have long to wait. The senior Mr. Gunsky rose to his feet, acknowledged the perfunctory applause, pulled a sheet of paper from his inside coat pocket, and after a few stillborn attempts at humor, started to read the list:

Robbins, notions, 96 per cent increase.

Lloyd, photography, 92 per cent increase.

Jesperson, toilet goods....

John sat there appalled. When Hank Robbins walked up to Mr. Gunsky, smiling all over, to get his check, he didn't even applaud. Why, Hank had only shown a gain of 30 per cent during the first three months of the contest!

He sat glumly through the rest of the program, listening to Mr. Gunsky heap glowing compliments on the head of Hank Robbins. No mention, of course, of the fact that he had bettered his previous record by five percentage points.

The meeting broke up and John headed for home. Coming up the front walk in the dark, he stumbled over Danny's skates, but caught himself on the railing to the steps before he could fall. If he had told Danny once about leaving his toys around, he had told him a thousand times! He stormed up the steps and into the front room, to find Danny in the big leather chair watching television. Seeing his favorite chair occupied by a sprawling seven-year-old was just too much. It was as though something had clicked in his brain. He reached out and grasped the startled boy by the scruff of the neck and dragged him from the chair over to the front door. He threw open the door and shoved him out into the night.

"When you've put those skates where they belong," he said, thickly, "you can come in and go right up to bed. And if I catch you leaving any of your toys around in the right-of-way again, so help me, I'll break every bone in your body!"

With this, he slammed the door and strode over to flop down in his chair breathing heavily.

*   *   *

Jim Clancy "anesthetized" his hostility with alcohol, Nora Kurz expressed hers through gossiping, Ted DuBois worked his off in playing a wild game of poker, and John Lloyd took out his on Danny. These are four of the many relatively mild ways of expressing hostility indirectly—that is, *not* toward the persons who aroused the hostility in the first place. We all use them. For the most part, we do not think very highly of this kind of behavior—after all, such behavior is not very "reasonable" or "sensible," it does not get at the root of our problems, and it tends to worsen our relations with others instead of bettering them. Sublimation ranks much higher in our esteem, because through it we can get rid of our hostility without offending others or doing anything that we will be ashamed of later. On the other hand, the person who has been frustrated, irritated, offended, or injured in any way is not likely to stop and think how he might express the resulting hostility in a positive, socially acceptable form; he is more concerned about expressing or getting rid of the hostility than anything else. For the most part, we stay within the limits of minor sins and offenses, but a few of us cannot stay within these limits and so must be restrained by the forces of law and order or of social opinion.

*   *   *

As Jerry Ames got in his car to drive to work that morning, he was still seething. Why Helen had to ruin every breakfast with an argument was more than he ever understood. This morning she had brought up the matter of his trip to New York again, after it had all been settled. For twelve years he had never missed a convention, and just because he was married to Helen he wasn't going to stop now. After all, a man was entitled to some recreation, and the way things were going, he'd be on the National Board in a couple of years or so.

He stepped on the starter. It turned over, but the engine failed to catch. He jazzed the gas pedal a couple of times and tried again. No luck. He started to swear and then looked at the ignition key. No wonder. Hadn't turned it on. He switched it on and tried again. Flooded.

Five minutes later, he backed the car out of the garage. Five minutes late on this of all mornings. Whatever happened, he couldn't afford to be late with Mr. Hotchkiss. "Kiss-of-Death" Hotchkiss they called him and with good cause. A sense of urgency settled on him as he sped down Holland Lane, well over the 25 mile limit. A few minutes later he eased himself into the teeming traffic on the Parkway. Fifty miles an hour was the average speed on the Parkway, but you could made sixty if you watched your chances. Jerry was an old hand at this "open-field running," as he like to call it, and this morning he dodged in and out in an attempt to make up the lost five minutes.

He tried to think of what he would tell Old Man Hotchkiss if he was late, but he couldn't get Helen out of his mind. That Helen could made you feel like a perfect heel without even raising her voice above a conventional tone. Some day, by God.... His hands shook a little as he gripped the wheel. A space opened up on his right as a car turned off the Parkway and he saw an opportunity to pick up a couple of hundred yards. Automatically, without giving it any thought, he moved into the right hand lane. A split second later there was the sound of squealing brakes, followed by a horn blast. Jerry had narrowly avoided hitting another car that had come up from behind on his right. The close call gave him a tight feeling around his stomach and he forgot about Helen and Mr. Hotchkiss for moment. But then, he thought, "If Helen hadn't nagged at me over breakfast this morning, I probably would have noticed that other car. It's a miracle I don't kill myself driving to work, the way she gets me started off in the morning on the wrong foot. What can you *do* with a dame like that?"

As he thought about what he would like to tell Helen, his mouth settled into a grim line, and he speeded up a little more. There was another open space in the center lane of traffic. Out of the corner of his eye he could see another car coming up fast in the inside land in preparation to move in, so he gave his car a little more power and cut in sharply. The driver behind him in the center lane gave him a sharp blast on the horn.

"Aw, keep your shirt on," he muttered to nobody in particular.

The car that he had nosed out had dropped back and another car was coming up in the inside lane. It drew abreast of him and stayed there. Jerry was wondering why it did not pass when he gave it a sideways glance. Then he knew why. It was a state police car with two policemen in the front seat. The one closer to him had the window down. He was pointing up ahead and saying something. Jerry couldn't hear him but he knew that the officer was telling him to pull over into the next turn-out place. He nodded dumbly, slowed down, and started to move over to the right. He felt limp as a rag, with all the fight gone out of him. No doubt about it—this was going to be one hell of a day....

*   *   *

What we have tried to do in this chapter is to show how hostility may express itself in a wide variety of forms. Since, as we have implied, it is important for leaders to cope with hostility among those they supervise or guide, it is equally important that they be able to identify hostility in whatever form it takes. This does not mean that leaders should go out "looking for trouble" or that they should be unduly concerned or upset when they come upon the evidence of hostility. As a group, leaders are probably oversensitive to the *direct* expression of hostility, but are likely to ignore or depreciate the importance of hostility that is expressed passively or indirectly. In reality, some forms of direct hostility may be relatively harmless or may even be turned to the advantage of the organization, whereas some forms of indirect or passive hostility may have a detrimental effect.

Leaders and others in authority must also recognize that hostility is a normal and natural reaction to frustrating situations and that it is a mistake to deny outlets for its expression. Thus the ever-present problem of leadership and authority revolves around hostility: identifying it, accepting it, finding its causes, and helping subordinates and group members find ways to express it that are useful, creative, and in the best interests of the group or organization.

CHAPTER FIVE

Patterns of Leadership and Authority

We have made a particular point in previous chapters of the fact that much of the hostility expressed toward a leader is not aroused directly by him, but is produced in part by the emotional conflicts and childhood experiences of subordinates and group members and by tradition or custom. We have used this emphasis in order to counterbalance our natural tendency to look everywhere but in ourselves for the cause of our feelings. In other words, when we are irritated or bored, we are inclined to blame the person who seems to be causing the irritation or boredom and are not inclined to investigate the part *we* are playing in bringing about these unpleasant emotional states.

However, we should be somewhat less than realistic if we implied that hostility directed toward leaders is caused solely by the feelings of subordinates and group members. Hence we shall in this chapter explore some of the more general aspects of what we have come to know as the "leader type of person," or, rather, the *types* of leader personalities, for our own hostility or acceptance of an authority figure depends to a large extent on the role he plays or the kind of person he is as well as on our own tendencies to resist or to accept direction and control.

There are many ways in which we could slice up the role of the leader to examine it more closely. Such a dissection can be very helpful, although there is always the danger in a discussion of this kind that the classifications will become too complex and that the thread of our analysis will be lost. Hence, it may serve our purpose better to start with the functions served by leaders in meeting the needs of the groups or organizations which they lead or direct.

Every group or organization has these two basic needs which must be met if it is to survive:

1. It must provide purpose and meaning for its members.

2. It must find ways to translate purpose and meaning into action.

Unless people have a need to form themselves into a group or to affiliate with existing groups, they will not willingly become involved, and if a group no longer has any meaning for its members, its effectiveness is at an end. And unless a group is able to carry out its functions, it must either find new purposes or end its existence as a group.

All groups must have leadership or direction in order to meet these needs. Even those groups that appear to be exceptions to this rule actually select members to serve in various key roles. Someone has to analyze the problems facing the group, someone has to initiate action, encourage, support, accept, criticize—in short, perform the role and function of the leader or director.

In order to make it possible for the groups they head to meet these two basic needs, leaders must perform any or all of three functions: 1) interpret the group's meaning to the membership; 2) help the group to make necessary changes, to adjust; and 3) help the group to remain the same, to resist changes or threats.

Now let us see how these functions would be performed by the leader of a small, prehistoric clan, a man we shall call Poppa.

To begin with, the members of this clan know *who they are*—they are the children of Poppa. This essential and basic fact gives them something in common and binds them together in a mutual society. And they have found out, largely through Poppa's guidance, that all around them is unknown territory filled with creeping death. It is best for them to stay close together. Therefore, being a member of the clan and being together with the clan means safety, and Poppa is the *symbol* of that safety. He *means* safety and protection to the members of the clan. Perhaps he has organized them into a fighting group that has withstood the attacks of wild animals or neighboring clans or perhaps he has led them to safety in times of flood or fire. Whatever he has done, he has communicated the idea to the clan that *Poppa means safety and security.*

Poppa also means *food and shelter.* He organizes the clan to gather fruits and nuts and tells them what is edible and what is not. He directs their hunting and fishing. He also directs the construction of shelter and designates when and where fires shall be built.

If anyone in the clan should ask why something is done, Poppa has the answers. We are attacking the clan next door because they are planning to attack us. We are hunting on the east side of the mountain today because it is bad luck to hunt on the other side. We always make a certain gesture when we light a fire because it keeps the fire spirits from biting us.

Poppa helps the clan to *make changes* and adapt themselves to their environment when he proposes that they move to a drier part of the forest, or when he decides that a new god or spirit should be included in their ritual, or when he tells the young men to raid the neighboring clans to find wives. On the other hand, he helps the clan to maintain its status quo and *resist change* by teaching and supervising rituals, by seeing that no strange elements or innovations are introduced, by punishing violations of the laws and customs of the clan, or by showing the young men how to defend themselves and the clan against attack.

One day one of the young men was offended because Poppa would not let him go hunting with the others but instead made him stay near the camp and help the women gather firewood. This latter task was a kind of punishment meted out by Poppa because he felt that the young man was too outspoken. The young man sulked for a while after this humiliation and then began to talk to some of the other clansmen.

He suggested that they could get a better leader than Poppa. He supported his claim by listing all the times that Poppa had erred in his judgment and had offended the spirits. The clansmen were disturbed at this talk, and some of the older men were angry. While they were arguing, Poppa walked in their midst and asked to know who was causing the disturbance. The young man stood up, beat his chest, and called upon Poppa to yield his position as leader of the clan, saying that Poppa had offended the spirits. Poppa told the young man that he must leave the tribe or stay and do woman's work. The young man's reply was to rush at Poppa with raised javelin. Poppa parried the thrust, and the two of them began a lengthy duel. The rest of the clan sat silently around, watching intently, for they knew that the winner would head the clan.

The young man seemed to have the advantage at first, because he was strong and aggressive. But Poppa was fast and tricky. Eventually, the young man grew tired of fencing and parrying and made a vicious lunge at Poppa, who neatly sidestepped the thrust and impaled his antagonist. As the young man sank down in death, Poppa turned his back and walked away to his hut, leaving the clan to drag the body of the young man off for burial.

And so Poppa helped the group to resist change—by keeping himself in power.

If the duel had turned out differently and the young man had won, he might have changed some of the meanings of the group and reinterpreted its purposes and functions. And here we have two kinds of leadership, each of which gives a different emphasis to the three functions we mentioned earlier. One kind of leadership we shall term dynamic, and the other, administrative, using these two terms in their looser sense. The dynamic leader is largely concerned with bringing about action and change of some sort. He is aggressive and forceful and is likely to back up his claims with an "appeal to reason," as the young man did when he listed the errors and deficiencies of Poppa. He likes to deal with present problems and simple, direct solutions. The administrative leader, on the other hand, is concerned with organizing and maintaining the group in order that it may continue to meet its goals and serve its purposes. The administrative leader is reluctant to change the goals and purposes of the group, whereas the dynamic leader may attack both the purposes and goals and the methods used in attaining them.

In modern life the dynamic leader becomes a Hitler or a Mussolini at one end of the spectrum or a Ghandi or an Abraham Lincoln at the other. Administrative leaders do not attract as much notice as do dynamic leaders, but there are more of them. Perhaps Calvin Coolidge, Pontius Pilate, and John Adams are reasonably good examples of administrative leaders. The accounting officer who believes that the organization exists so that he may keep records, and the board member who opposes a needed move merely because it has never been done, are good negative examples of administrative leadership, whereas the executive who helps to maintain his company at a high level of efficiency and productivity, and makes it a satisfying place in which to work, is a good example of positive administrative leadership.

In the primitive example we have given, Poppa is largely an adminstrative leader because he is principally interested in maintaining the status quo. If he is a particularly wise and perceptive man, he may make helpful changes in the organization and administration of his clan. The chances are, however, that change is a frightening thing to him, which means that he will fight to the death to maintain his small world just as it is. The young man is, of course, a symbol for dynamic leadership. Like many dynamic leaders, even today, he is not very sure what he is *for*, but he knows very well what he is *against*—Poppa. When Poppa was a young man, he was a dynamic leader. He rebelled against the established order in his clan and founded a clan of his own. He was an active force in bringing about change. But now he is in his declining years and he wants to keep what he has, both for himself and for the clan.

There are many other patterns of leadership to be found among primitive tribes, of course. Tribes that move around a lot and are warlike and attracted to lives of violence and passion tend to produce leaders of the dynamic sort, whereas tribes that remain in one spot, and are peaceful and agriculturally minded are more inclined to develop leaders of the administrative type. Most tribes and nations develop both kinds of leaders, with a preponderance in one direction or another, depending on their way of life—turbulent or peaceful.

The history of our own Western culture shows the effect of these trends. The growth of the Roman Empire depended in part on the dynamic leadership of its generals and its political reformers and in part on the ability of its administrators. Probably the latter played the more dominant role. History has seen the rise and fall of many military rulers. The Romans differ from most because they were able to organize and administer the colonies and provinces they conquered. In this way, they consolidated their gains and perpetuated the Empire. There was enough dynamic leadership among the Romans to keep the Empire growing and adjusting to internal and external changes. It thus developed enough size and strength to resist the twin dangers of disintegration and military defeat. When the Empire failed to develop dynamic leadership, it passed into the hands of the barbarians from the north and east who did not lack for dynamic leadership.

The violent period that followed the collapse of the Empire was marked by the rise and fall of a succession of leaders, mostly of the dynamic type.

The feudal system developed around leaders of the dynamic sort, powerful, vigorous men who were able to give protection and a measure of security to the peasants and lesser nobility in their neighborhood. As time went on, and more and more administrative leadership emerged, these neighborhoods tended to grow larger and larger, and their leaders in turn were themselves included in duchies, bishoprics, and kingdoms. This process reached its peak development during the Middle Ages when leaders of the administrative type dominated and were able to bring about a high degree of stability to at least the internal relationships of nations and communities.

The 16th century saw a reaction to domination by administrative leaders, and a new group of dynamic leaders—religious, political, scientific, and literary—appeared on the scene. Their accomplishments—popularly referred to as the Renaissance—were in turn organized, developed, and systematized by administrative leaders, many of whom tended to be more concerned with adminstration and regulation than with purpose and function.

If there has been a trend during these two thousand or so years, it has been that administrative leaders have been gaining more power and authority, are becoming more numerous, and are maintaining their influence for longer periods. As civilizations grow and develop, there is an increased need for administrative leaders and a corresponding decrease in the need for dynamic leaders. Dynamic leaders fit best into primitive surroundings where there is need for rapid decisions and drastic action to deal with immediate dangers and crises. Dynamic leaders are good persons to have on hand during emergencies. But what civilizations try to do is eliminate emergencies, or at least make them predictable enough so that one can be prepared for them.

What has happened, therefore, is that the kinds of emergencies primitive man had to face have almost disappeared and have been replaced by problems of great complexity, but problems which can be met successfully, for the most part, through use of the organizational and administrative arrangements of today. For example, when primitive man was hungry, he went out and gathered food or hunted it. If he was successful, he ate; if unsuccessful, he starved. Today, getting food is a relatively less important problem among the many problems we have on our minds. It is really a part of a larger complex of problems. It involves working for money, exchanging the money for food, and preparing and serving the food in accordance with local customs. In order for the food to be available in the stores and markets, it must pass through a number of stages, both economic and physical, before it is available for purchase or consumption. If this sounds less efficient than the methods of primitive man, let us be reminded that our system provides us with food on a far more dependable basis. Whereas primitive man was constantly at the mercy of the forces of nature, one of the chief contributions of civilization has been to place these forces partly under the control of man, or at least to erect a buffer between man and nature. And the maintenance of this protection against nature is largely the responsibility of administrative leaders. This is a relatively routine problem, one that does not challenge the imagination of the dynamic leader in the modern world to the extent that it did in the primitive world.

When the production or distribution of food threatens to become a problem, we try to solve it through administrative methods and include it as one of the many problems we have on our agenda. When hunger is a really acute problem, as it is in many parts of the world today, administrative leaders often fail to bring about the desired solution, either because solving the problem would bring about too many changes in the status quo or because they do not know how to introduce technological changes. In either event, dynamic leaders find such conditions attractive to the development and use of their talents. Thus it is in the poor or underdeveloped nations that most of the world's dynamic leaders are to be found today. Unfortunately, they appear to be more interested in politics than in economics and devote their energy to power struggles, rather than to raising living standards. Those developing countries who have been most successful are those whose economic development has been fostered by leaders of the administrative type.

What we have seen in this brief historical review is a change from situations that could be controlled by the physical strength, commanding qualities, and emotional appeal of a single individual directing the efforts of a relatively small group to situations that must be controlled through close coordination, long-range planning, research, organization, and the development of complex networks of communication. These latter functions are directed most efficiently by administrative leaders. This change means also that the power which was concentrated in the hands of the dynamic leader is now distributed through the hands of an endless number of administrative leaders. And this power is increasingly being derived by them from the people who benefit by its use rather than from a few individuals who have been able to seize or accumulate power. Thus the older picture of the leader who owed his position to his ability to terrorize, charm, manipulate, or merely to be in the right spot at the right time is giving way to the leader who owes his position to his ability to manage situations for the benefit of a large number of people, the larger the better.

We can see this trend in the history of our own country during the last half century. The economic life of our country at the turn of the century was dominated by such dynamic figures as J.P. Morgan, Andrew Carnegie, and Mark Hanna who were able to accumulate vast amounts of economic power by their ability to manipulate people and property. Today the business aristocrat (and autocrat) of the 1900's has largely given way to the manager, the individual who is able to organize and direct the activities of large and complex organizations on behalf of thousands of stockholders and for the benefit of millions of customers. The business manager of today thus finds it necessary, by reason of the demands made on him, to be concerned more and more about his responsibilities to other people and less and less about self-interests.

*   *   *

Although the heyday of the dynamic leader has passed, this does not mean there is no place for him in today's world. There are two distinct functions or jobs that he can perform better than the administrative leader.

For one thing, administrative leaders are not always in agreement on how to manage the world. There are differences of opinion and conviction. In this country (and undoubtedly in others) there are, for example, two schools of thought on social welfare. One group of administrative leaders believes that social welfare services provided by the government and supported by taxation should be expanded; another group believes that they should be held to a minimum. Whether they are expanded or reduced in any given period will depend in part upon the persuasion of the dynamic leaders that the country selects to formulate policy. The making of policy tends to be a dynamic function; the translation of policy into action and making it effective is an administrative function. Where leadership is lacking in dynamic qualities, it attempts to avoid making decisions. Sometimes the postponement of decisions is a wise move, but many administrative leaders lack the courage to make difficult and unpopular decisions. Unable to face the hostility that might be aroused by an unpopular decision, they prefer to let matters drift.

When minimal leadership prevails, some people are able to "muddle through," as the British say, and find ways of resolving or living with difficult situations. But sometimes problems escalate, situations deteriorate, and people become discouraged, panicky, and disorganized. Such conditions are likely to produce charismatic leaders, like Hitler and Churchill, both of whom had dynamic qualities that appealed to millions of their fellow countrymen. The fact that emergency situations produced two such different kinds of leaders is due in part to the emotional climate and cultural style of the two countries.

The second function that the dynamic leader can perform better than the administistative leader is that of interpretation. Back near the beginning of the chapter we mentioned interpretation as one of the key roles of the leader. A leader must be able to meet the need that his followers have for *purpose*—they must have purposes that bring and hold them together. When the group becomes frightened or frustrated or discouraged, it begins to doubt the reasons for its existence. The individual members begin to wonder if they would not be better off acting and thinking for themselves alone and "let the group go hang!" Or they begin to believe (sometimes with reason) that certain members of the group are benefiting by the crisis that faces the group.

And so they look for a leader who can say to them convincingly, *"You* are the people who can solve this problem. *You* have the ability, provided you work together under my direction. *I* can lead you on to success (or victory, or security, or whatever). Let me remind you that you are chosen people (or whatever) and chosen people can do anything!"

If the leader is successful in his appeal, it is because he has been able to tell the people "who they are" (chosen people who can do anything), reassure them about their adequacy and competency (provided they work together), and designate himself as the person who can best help them to work together. And he generally makes his appeals even more convincing by attacking the persons who are currently bungling the problems that need solution so badly. The greater the group's dissatisfaction with their current leadership, the greater his opportunity to be recognized as leader.

The dynamic leader may also make interpretations which are less popular but equally necessary. Examples of this kind of leadership are provided by persons like Jeremiah, Jesus of Nazareth, William Penn, and Voltaire, each of whom in his own unique way attacked the status quo and the administrative leadership of his day. Their words and deeds are recurring notes of dissent serving to remind the people of their day and this of the injustices, inconsistencies, and inhumanities that administrative leaders often perpetrate and perpetuate in their attempts to maintain the status quo and to avoid offending anyone.

For the last few pages, we have been talking as though dynamic and administrative leaders constitute two separate and mutually exclusive types of persons—that is, a given leader is either administrative *or* dynamic, but not both. We have done this largely by way of emphasis and contrast. In reality, of course, most leaders are something of both types.

The business autocrats of the early 1900's had great capacity for organization and administration, and most of their time and energy was spent in organizing and administering their economic empires. However, when we compare them to the business leaders of today, the former appear far more colorful and individualistic, more interested in producing *change,* than do the latter. On the other hand, the American business leader of today is inclined to be more dynamic, more venturesome, more interested in initiating change (in the shape of growth, development, and improvement of efficiency and productive capacity) than is the typical business leader of Europe.[1] The latter tends to be more administratively minded, more concerned with maintaining the status quo through building up cartels and marketing agreements. American business leadership is characterized by a willingness to expend energy with the expectation of creating new energy, whereas European leadership is more concerned with *conserving* human energy. Change and the promise of change tend to be attractive to Americans but are disturbing and threatening to Europeans.

Although Cameron Hawley published his novel, *Executive Suite*[2], in the 1950's, the picture it presents of the conflict between dynamically and administratively oriented leaders is as valid today as it was a generation ago. In the novel, the prize for which the hero and his chief antagonist strive is the presidency of a large furniture corporation which has just been vacated by the death of an aggressive, dynamic leader, a man who built up the company from bankruptcy. The hero is a dynamic individual, one who will carry on the expansionistic policies of the former president. His antagonist, the comptroller, wishes to maintain the business of the company at current levels, introducing economics to produce higher profits. His is the safe, sane, conservative approach. Nevertheless, the hero wins out, largely because of his ability to convince the board of directors that a business should be a growing, live thing, that attempts to make it static and retard its competitive expansion would not only lead to deterioration and decay but would also stifle the enthusiasm that people who participate in business need to make them productive and effective.

However, the dynamic leader is not universally popular. Surveys of executives in business and industry find them divided in their preferences for the kind of persons they wish in key positions in their firms. Presidents and top executives tend to be evenly divided as to whether they prefer men who are dynamic, vigorous, aggressive, and creative, to men who have administrative and organizational skill and who are able to get along with others easily. Personnel managers especially seem to prefer the second type of individual. This division of opinion reflects the fact that the dynamic leader is harder to get along with. He is more likely to be individualistic and opinionated, to be cantankerous and rebellious.[3] These qualities can be more easily tolerated in older executives who have reached the top of the status ladder. The junior executive who displays them is marked as a misfit and is forced to conform to the administrative pattern or to seek other fields of employment. The result is that business and industries are hard pressed when they come to look for top-drawer executives who are capable of original thinking and are not afraid to speak their minds.

Thus American business is faced with a constant dilemma. On the one hand, it needs the growth and development that can only be sparked by leaders with dynamic qualities, but, on the other hand, it needs the stability and harmony that is the contribution of the administrative leader.

*　　　*　　　*

The leaders of business are not alone in their dilemma, for it is one that is shared by the public at large.

The plain fact of the matter is that we are inclined, in our calmer moments, when not faced by emergencies, to be skeptical of dynamic leaders. Our skepticism has deep roots. One of them goes back into our middle-class heritage. The merchants and tradesmen who constituted the middle class during the Middle Ages and the Renaissance looked with disapproval on emotional display. Emotions only got you into trouble, they felt. Look at the difficulties encountered by the nobility, poets and musicians, and the peasantry. If these people would just be sensible, control their unseemly passions, and lead more orderly lives, they would be spared the troubles that continually beset them.

The middle class was particularly exercised about the ruling class, because their impulsive acts and whims affected the welfare of whole communities and nations. The worst of it was that the people of the middle class themselves found it difficult to withstand the charm, the enthusiasm, the stirring appeals, and the logic of these dynamic leaders. Sometimes the ruling classes led them wisely, but sometimes they led them into death, destruction, and bankruptcy. Middle-class people began to wonder whether they weren't being used and exploited by the ruling classes, and whether they couldn't run things better. As a result, they gradually took over the functions of government, which they conducted in a more pedestrian, less colorful and less individualistic fashion.

The members of the middle class were and still are managers and administrators. They began by managing their businesses and their cities and expanded their operations to include national governments. This shift in controls did not occur without bloodshed. We note, for example, the Roundhead Rebellion in England during the 17th century, our own Revolution, and the French Revolution. Even the American Civil War is in some respects a conflict between the middle-class, managerial interests of the Northern States and the aristocratic, individualistic (States' rights) interests of the Southern planter.

Nor did this change-over in direction and control proceed evenly. There were many times when middle-class people permitted themselves to be charmed or swayed by charismatic, dynamic leaders in the form of aristocrats, poets, soldiers, and religious leaders. These people created instabilities that in the end made life more difficult. To be sure, they also made it more interesting, and sometimes they solved problems that middle-class people wanted to ignore or overlook, but they were distracting influences. The middle-class person has traditionally admired reason and order. These leaders were persons of feeling and emotion, they were disturbing, they upset the established order of things. Not only did they make the worshipper of reason and order feel uncomfortable, but he also felt guilty when he succumbed to their persuasion.

On the other hand, even members of the middle class sometimes tire of their own drab respectability and grow impatient with their own cautiousness. When times are particularly difficult, they, too, join the growing chorus of complaint against inefficient and uncaring bureaucrats, political corruption, and failure of top leadership to deal with the pressing problems of the day. An example from recent history is the behavior of the middle-class merchants of Tehran, whose dissatisfaction with the Shah's government increased to the point that they threw in their lot with the Ayatollah Khomeini, the charismatic leader of the revolution.

*   *   *

Both administrative and dynamic leadership are potential sources of hostility. Dynamic leadership arouses hostility because of its tendency to center its appeal around the ideas of a single person or a small group. It tends to ignore the rights and feelings of the members of the larger group, regardless of whether the larger group is a small committee or whether it is a nation or a group of nations. Dynamic leadership can be unrealistic and irrational, and, because we can be persuaded thereby to do things that we later regret, we have good reason to be skeptical or suspicious about emotional appeals. When we feel that someone is attempting to appeal to us through our "weaker side"—that is, our emotions—we are likely to be doubly suspicious. And suspicion is very often a prelude to hostility.

Some of the hostility we may feel toward dynamic leaders is related to the hostility and anxiety we develop as a result of growing up in a family. Dynamic leaders sometimes play a parental role with respect to their subordinates. Even if they do not act in ways that are obviously parentlike, subordinates may nevertheless react to them much as they would their own parents. Some subordinates may respond to a leader in accepting but essentially dependent ways, reenacting the roles they played as children, but others may reenact the "authority problems" of their adolescence. As a result, they react with hostility even to reasonable attempts to direct, control, or monitor their activities.

Administrative leaders also arouse hostility in a variety of ways. Again, some of our anxieties and misgivings about losing our identity in a group can be focused on administrative leaders in the form of hostility and resentment. It is true that administrative leaders help to bring about orderliness and efficiency, but sometimes we do not *feel* like being orderly or efficient. At such times, we become very impatient with administrative leaders and their demands on us. We also get impatient with them when they do not produce results or solutions fast enough. Administrative leaders do not get ahead of the group, as dynamic leaders sometimes do. They are more likely to lag *behind* the group; hence we are likely to resent their inability to keep up with us, particularly when events move along rapidly and changes take place with increasing speed. Administrative leaders always seem to be recommending caution and deliberation when we want to move ahead rapidly.

One of the most frustrating qualities possessed by administrative leaders is their anonymity. They lack color and individuality; they are responsible to the larger organization rather than directly to us, their followers. Therefore, it is difficult to place the blame on some particular person when something goes wrong or when problems are not met quickly and efficiently. Because of this difficulty, we are forced to focus our hostility on "the system," "red tape," or "bureaucracy." We do not like this business of having to deal with a vague, indefinable, intangible entity. We like to have our problems solved in a simple, direct way on a person-to-person basis, and because this is what we expect and hope for, we are so often doomed to frustration and disappointment. In the first place, problems grow more complex with every decade[4], and in the second place, persons who try to make a significant impression on today's pressing problems—inflation or crime in the streets, to name two examples—find that their ability to bring about the changes that are needed is severely restricted, to say the least.

Let's say that you accidentally run into a neighbor and damage the fender of his automobile. The simple, direct way to deal with the problem would be for the two of you to decide who was responsible and have him pay the cost. But, instead, the insurance companies of the two motorists are notified, and bids for repairing the fender are sought. A bid is accepted, the fender repaired, and the repairman is paid. But in order to achieve this, a dozen or more people become involved: adjusters, typists, filing clerks, bookkeepers,and perhaps even the brokers who sold the insurance in the first place. And the record of the accident becomes part of a staggering array of statistical data used by the insurance companies to figure their profit and loss and to calculate rates for coming years. We have erected this vast, complex structure of persons and processes in order to protect ourselves against unexpected expenses and to share risks involved in using automobiles. We certainly do not want to rid ourselves of automobile insurance, of course, even though using it involves delays and prevents direct, immediate solutions to problems. Yet, at times, it is hard to accept the fact that the world is growing so increasingly complex and that a great deal of what we call red tape and bureaucracy is inevitable.

In spite of our tendency to grow impatient and suspicious of both administrative and dynamic leadership, most of us would admit that they are a necessary part of living in a world composed almost entirely of other people. We need both kinds of leadership, of course—dynamic leadership, to appeal to the human spirit and make us want to do the things that should be done, and administrative leadership, to help us organize in meeting our own goals efficiently and effectively and to provide the security and stability we all need. And the most effective leader is neither all dynamic nor all administrative, but one who is both, particularly one who has a certain flexibility, one who can help us develop the organizational structure we must have to carry out our goals, but one who can also provide the inspirational spark of dynamic leadership when *it* is needed.

FOOTNOTES CHAPTER 5

[1]See J.J. Servan-Schreiber, *The American Challenge*; Atheneum. 1979.
[2]Boston: Houghton Mifflin, 1952.
[3]Studies made by myself and others show that creative people tend to be more nonconforming and ornery than others.
[4]See Alvin Toffler, *Future Shock*; Random House, 1970.

CHAPTER SIX

Power, Prestige, and the Aristocratic Tradition

One of the keys to understanding the hostility that leaders commonly arouse may be found in the relationship of leadership to power. One rather basic concept of a leader is that of a person who possesses power—more power, that is, than that those who are not leaders. To expand this concept, let us say that leaders are persons who accumulate, possess, use, dispense, and create power. By power, we mean the faculty of getting others to do things, willingly or unwillingly. And this is a clue to our hostility, because a leader is a person who can get us do things that we might not want to do. The more power a person has over us, the less freedom and individuality we have. The more power a person has over us, the weaker and more inadequate we feel by comparison. The more helpless we feel, the more anxious. We resent someone who has power because he can arouse our anxiety so easily.

Leaders are necessary because groups are necessary. We cannot do without them. Dispensing with the order and direction that leaders contribute to groups inevitably creates anarchy, a highly unstable and dangerous state of affairs. But the fact that leaders are necessary does not mean that we can easily accept this fact and thus dismiss as baseless and irrelevant the anxiety and hostility we feel toward them. Perhaps we would have been happier if we were more realistic, if we *could* relax and accept the need for control and conformity without question. Happier? Perhaps, but not better off. After all, our anxiety about the power of leaders helps to remind us to keep a careful watch on them so that they do not exceed their authority wittingly or unwittingly. But we *do* have to be concerned about keeping our anxieties from running away from us. If anxiety and hostility grow to unreasonable levels, they disrupt the efficient functioning of groups or organizations. On the other hand, we do not want to stifle our anxiety to the point that we are no longer sensitive to the presence of potential threats to our security and freedom that may lie hidden in the acts of our leaders.

There are some other reasons why the presence of power is likely to arouse hostility and anxiety among group members or subordinates. There is the matter of envy.[1] Many a person asks himself or wonders: "Why is *he* the president (or the chairman or the branch manager or whatever)? I'm just as good (or as well qualified or as able) as he is."

The feeling here is one of being deprived or cheated because someone else has been preferred for a position of power. It is as though something that was rightfully ours has been taken from us and placed beyond our reach. The roots of this feeling go back to the early days of our childhood. One of the easiest ways to provoke a child to anger is to take something away from him. The proverbial ease of taking candy from a baby holds true only if you can successfully ignore his screams of rage.

Being resentful of the promotion of another person, is of course, more or less a childish reaction, unless double-dealing and dishonesty were actually involved. Yet most of us are not as emotionally mature as we would like to be; hence envy of a leader's power is not uncommon.

Sometimes envy of people having power or authority becomes obsessive.[2] There are some, for example, who seem to be in a chronic state of alarm, accusing any and every leader or administrator of being self-serving, concerned only with defending and expanding his or her power or privilege. Obsessive envy occasionally reaches the point where it interferes with an individual's relationship not only with authority figures, but with other group or organization members as well. However, our concern here is not with such exaggerated (though not uncommon) symptoms, but with the relatively widespread undercurrent of envious resentment that is characteristically present in any organization or working group. It commonly surfaces when one member of a group is promoted or is otherwise singled out for recognition. On such an occasion, those who are especially envious may express their unhappiness openly and directly, as Ed did, when Howard Galvin approached him with a message from top management. (See Chapter I.)

Many of us are ambivalent about power, irrespective of whether we possess it or whether it is used on us by others. We wonder whether it is right and proper that a leader or an administrator have the right to require others to follow orders and to exact penalties for noncompliance, feeling that people should and probably *would* do the right thing *without being required to do so*. Voluntary controls thus have a great appeal for us. True, they often fail, but we generally feel better about requiring more stringent regulations after voluntary controls have been given a reasonable trial.

This reluctance about the use of power seems to have a rational basis. The great majority of the public are peaceful, law-abiding folk. If everyone were criminally inclined, there would not be enough policemen to keep us in line. There is, of course, far more crime on the streets that there ought to be, but nevertheless, the average person goes about his daily life in the reasonable expectation that he will not become a victim. The larger group that we call "society" is able to function in a relatively peaceful way because most of us have a mutual, tacit understanding that we will not engage in behavior that is detrimental to the safety and welfare of others. We do not need to be told to behave ourselves; we do so automatically, without giving it a second thought. It is because of this common experience of not needing power and not wanting to have power used on us that we are ambivalent—even negative—about its use. Government officials, and authority figures in general, we feel, should get along without recourse to power, and many of us would like to see their powers reduced.

Our ambivalence about power in the hands of authority figures has a long history. Much of the power that today is in the hands of the people has been taken from aristocracy in the course of struggles that have lasted for centuries.

The earliest leaders, the chiefs of primitive tribes and clans, like Poppa, whom we described in Chapter 5, were leaders by virtue of their ability to seize and hold power—by being strongest or by getting there first or both. Poppa is the leader because he is literally the father of the clan. He was there first with the greatest strength. And he remains in his position of leadership as long as he can defend it against all comers.

However, even primitive leaders did not depend upon power alone as the means of maintaining their positions. When a leader controls by power alone, he is successful only as long as he can defend his position or as long as he can give his followers reason to fear him. Therefore, if a leader wants to keep his position over a long period of time, he must somehow convey the idea to his followers that he *ought* to be the leader, that he is the *right person* to be the leader. When a leader has been able to convince his group on these points, he may be said to have *prestige* He is then no longer a leader by virtue of superior strength or wisdom or because of having been there first, but because of his *right* to leadership.

From the group's point of view, one can see how they would find such arguments persuasive, for there is a need to have continuity in leadership. Because of this need, the leader who is able to establish his prestige calls forth the *loyalty* of the group to him as their *legitimate* leader.

Probably in the most primitive societies, legitimacy and prestige were acquired by those who arose to positions of leadership by happenstance— by being there first or by possessing superior strength. But after a while, leaders found new ways of achieving supremacy and power and maintaining them through developing prestige. One of the commonest ways of acquiring prestige was to develop oneself as a *symbol* of the group. In other words, Chief Bowstring of the Hunter tribe might exercise power over his followers not necessarily because he was the strongest, but rather because he was their *chief*. Chief Bowstring *represented* them; he stood for them; his presence or existence gave the group *meaning*. In a similar way, the British Crown gave meaning to the citizens of the Empire. Being subjects of the Queen gave them a feeling of kinship with the people next door, as well as with the people in parts of the Empire they had never seen. One of the deepest and most pervasive needs we have is to be assured of "who we are." And the people of the Empire knew that whoever else they might be, they were subjects of the Queen. For them she has the maximum in prestige.

Primitive leaders, like many leaders and rulers today, were able to develop a wide variety of devices to support their legitimacy and prestige. One of these methods was to claim that the gods or the spirits approved of one's leadership. If one could insure one's position by becoming a priest and leading the tribe in worship, so much the better. Even primitive tribes developed specialities, however, and as a result it was common for one person to be the military leader of the tribe and for another to be the religious leader. Between them, they either shared the political power or squabbled over it. What often happened was that the military leader lent his power to the religious leader, and the religious leader assured the people of the legitimacy of the military leader. In other words, there was an exchange of physical or military power for symbolic power (prestige).

*   *   *

As civilizations developed more stability, it became customary for leaders to devise means of insuring that their descendants be maintained in positions of leadership. Thus we see the development of a nobility or aristocracy. An aristocracy, be it understood, maintains its position of leadership by virtue of the fact that it is composed of "the best people"—the Greek word "aristos" means, in fact, "the best."

Aristocrats maintained their positions of leadership through a variety of devices and conventions. For example, they encouraged the idea that the children of leaders should make the best candidates for leadership, because they had presumably inherited the qualities that made their parents such acceptable leaders. Furthermore, they were *legitimate*, they had *prestige*, and it was disloyal and treasonous for any upstart to declare that he had a better right to the leadership. Any claim that a rebel might make that the gods or the spirits were on his side would be regarded with a great deal of suspicion, since the religious hierarchy had very likely already endorsed the ruling family.

Theoretically, this reduced the turnover in leadership and increased stability and security. However, no system that involves human relationships works perfectly. Sometimes aristocrats perpetrated cruel injustices and exploited and weakened their followers to the point that they themselves were swallowed up by rebellion or by competing tribes and nations. Sometimes religious leaders disapproved of ruling families and withdrew their endorsement, thus reducing their prestige and rendering them vulnerable to overthrow and rebellion.

One device we have not mentioned, one which was (and still is) used by the aristocracy in order to maintain and to perpetuate their hold on positions of leadership, is that of wealth. Wealth is an economic form of power. Wealth is a means of controlling people without recourse to physical force. Leaders very early used wealth as a supplementary means of exercising power and found it to be a useful way of perpetuating one's rule. A dying leader could leave his wealth to his children who could then use it as a means of establishing themselves as leaders.

During the earlier, more or less agricultural stages of our civilization, wealth and aristocracy were synonymous. The aristocracy controlled the land and the land produced the wealth. However, with the development of cities, manufacturing, and trade, a merchant class developed that possessed economic power but not prestige. Merchants occupied an intermediate position between the aristocracy and the peasantry. Sometimes they (or their children) "joined" the aristocracy by becoming landowners, by buying titles, or by marrying impoverished aristocrats. But this middle-class group grew too rapidly to become absorbed by the aristocracy and eventually, during the 16th century, they began to challenge the rights of the aristocracy to monopolize the positions of leadership. They began to question whether the ability to rule and to lead was inherited, for it seemed to them that these were *skills that could be learned* like any other skills. After all, they had achieved some success in governing themselves through city councils and guilds.

This discovery—that leadership could be learned—marked the beginning of the end of the monopoly the aristocrat exercised over positions of leadership. The claims of the middle class became more persistent and insistent. Furthermore, the expanding empires, the increasing complexity of warfare, and the changing world economy all demanded more leadership and more kinds of specialized managerial skills than could be supplied by the aristocracy. The idea that the skills of leadership could be learned and that education and leadership went hand in hand grew and developed. And so we have come to believe today that everyone should have free and equal opportunity to exercise leadership. This is one of the basic principles that underlie our system of free public education.

*   *   *

In modern America, we have not entirely abandoned the idea that aristocrats make good leaders. We still tend to give special attention to members of leading families when it comes to selecting persons for high positions in politics and business. Programs for civic betterment find rough going unless they are endorsed by leading figures in the community. We do not carry this idea to the point that such endorsement insures the success of the undertaking. Although endorsement by persons of prestige does not insure the success of civic undertakings, the lack of such endorsement is likely to result in failure.

It is difficult to tell whether the prestige of our homegrown aristocracy will wax or wane. Rapid changes in our economic and political life make it increasingly difficult for aristocrats to accumulate wealth and political power, and our present tax laws are a distinct threat to the development of inherited fortunes. However, education has developed a prestige of its own. It is becoming more and more essential for a candidate for a position of leadership, large or small, to have a college education. This is not a requirement that we always consciously look for when we select leaders, but it appears to be one that operates effectively nevertheless, as witness the fact that an ever-increasing proportion of our leaders in business and public life are college graduates. Nor is the aristocratic flavor entirely absent here, for the higher the position of leadership, the greater the likelihood that the occupant attended one of the smaller, more select liberal arts colleges like Oberlin, Reed, or Haverford, or one of the Ivy League institutions like Harvard, Yale, or Princeton.

In today's world, status, prestige, and income are derived largely from one's occupation, and occupational level is determined largely by the amount of education one has. There tends to be a rough division between those jobs that demand a college education and those that do not. Hence in America, as well as in other industrialized countries, a dual-class system is emerging, one that is composed of a college-educated dominant class and a less-educated under class. The terms "white collar" and "blue collar" are often applied to these two groups, but the terms tend to blur the distinction between them. For one thing, many white-collar workers—typists, file clerks, cashiers, salespeople, and the like—are not college-educated, as a general rule. They tend to share many of the interests and values of the under class and do not have the status or prestige of members of the dominant class—accountants, teachers, clergy, and engineers, for instance.

Members of the under class often express mixed feelings about being supervised, directed, advised, or governed by the college-educated members of the dominant group. These "consumers" of leadership point out that college does not really teach people how to manage the affairs of others and express doubts as to whether anything practical or reality-oriented is or can be taught by college professors. They therefore question the suitability of a college background as a prerequisite of leadership and authority. People in institutions of higher education of course brand this attitude as "antiintellectualism" and regard it as one of the reasons why state-supported colleges and universities are inadequately funded by legislative bodies.

Educated people are ordinarily unaware that they are the target of smouldering resentment in the under class. Sometimes this resentment finds its expression in the defeat of a political candidate who has been labeled as an "intellectual" or a "liberal." The resentment may also flare up in labor-management disputes. Some members of the under class receive higher wages than college-educated employees in the same organization—janitors may be paid more than school teachers, for instance—but they nevertheless feel insecure and defensive in dealing with them, fearful that educated people will manipulate and exploit them if given a chance.

The feeling is also widespread among under class employees that management personnel, most of whom are college-educated, do not understand the needs and problems of the people they supervise. This situation is of long standing. A generation ago, the pioneer industrial psychologist, F.J. Roethlisberger[3], wrote of the breakdown in communication between workers and their college-educated supervisors. Management personnel and workers simply do not speak the same language, a fact that is concealed from their awareness by the steadfast belief that the other group *must certainly* understand. Many a supervisor has asked, sarcastically, when faced by a failure to carry out his orders, "What's the matter—don't you understand English?" The fact of the matter is that more-educated and less-educated people use different forms of language—different words and descriptive terms and of course different pronunciations. And there is much in any attempt at communication that is sketchy and vague, that takes for granted that the listener will know what concepts are referred to.

Thus management people and workers are mutually frustrated in their attempts to communicate with each other, and each group accuses the other either of not wanting to understand or of understanding but being too selfish or stubborn to cooperate.

Much of this difficulty in communication is related to the fact that things appear differently to employers and employees. Even though one has been an employee, once one becomes a manager, events and situations at work take on a different meaning. For example, one becomes more concerned about the long-range implications of the problems met at work. But above and beyond this basic difference in viewpoint, getting a college education does bring about certain changes that make communication with persons of less education more difficult. College-educated people may try to explain this away or resolve not to let it happen to them, but it exists nevertheless. Fortunately, there are ways of dealing with this difficulty, ways that we shall discuss when we take up the general problem of communication and the method of the democratic group decision.

FOOTNOTES CHAPTER 6

[1]For an excellent analysis of envy, as well as a discussion of its positive social value, see Helmut Schoeck, *Envy: A Theory of Social Behavior*; Harcourt, Brace, Jovanovich, 1970.

[2]Studies conducted by me and my coresearchers, using tests that tap motives lying below ordinary awareness, suggest that feelings of envy, suspicion, and apprehensiveness regarding authority figures characteristically run higher in underdeveloped countries than in the United States and Canada, especially in countries where tradition requires that persons in authority receive a high degree of deference from those ranking lower on the social scale.

[3]*Management and Morale*; Harvard University Press, 1941.

CHAPTER SEVEN

Patterns of Authority, Old and New

We have all been made conscious at times of the vast differences that exist among the various kinds of people who guide, direct, or supervise our activities. Some of them are likable and incur little hostility; others are disliked. Much of this difference in acceptance is due to the personalities of the persons involved, but some of it is the result of the kind of leadership roles they display. In other words, whether an authority figure is liked or disliked depends partly on the *pattern of influence* he uses. What we plan to do in this chapter is to discuss four common patterns. Although most authority figures defy absolute classification into any single type, most of them nevertheless show basic tendencies in one of the four directions we shall describe.

The first type of person in authority we shall discuss is the "parental figure"—that is, the individual who acts or behaves in a parent-like manner, who expects himself to be treated like a parent, and who is expected by his subordinates to behave like a parent.

The authority figure or leader who plays a parental role is expected to know all or most of the answers and to be able to control and direct the activities of his followers or subordinates. He expects their loyalty, and they expect protection, help, or direction from him. Most of the authority figures or leaders we encounter in everyday life play variations on the parental theme, at least part of the time. This holds true for employers, administrators, executives, teachers, policemen, lawyers, dentists, social workers, and the clergy, as well as an endless list of other people who play roles involving leadership or authority.

There are two main types of parental roles. One involves the dominating, forbidding, punishing, forthright, and directive behavior that is consistent with the image of the "father figure." The other involves nourishing, supporting, reassuring, understanding, and sheltering behavior that is consistent with the image of the "mother figure." Mother- or father-figure roles can be played by authority figures of either sex, of course.

Most authority figures play both types of roles with varying degrees of emphasis. Sometimes the positions they occupy appear to demand the more dominant father-type behavior; sometimes the more sympathetic mother qualities seem appropriate. Personal qualities of the authority figures are important: some prefer a paternalistic stance; others favor more maternalistic approaches. Even leaders and administrators who do not enjoy mother- or father-type roles are manipulated into playing them by the people they supervise. Although we may say that we resent paternalistic or maternalistic treatment, we may send forth unconscious signals suggesting how we really want persons in authority to deal with us.

The feelings we have as adults regarding individuals in positions of authority are determined in large degree by the attitudes we had as children and adolescents toward our parents. If we were inclined to lean on our parents during childhood and look to them as our main source of love, appreciation, and security, then we are likely to look upon authority figures in the same light. If, on the other hand, we were inclined to rebel against our parents, to resent any attempts to restrict our liberties, and to be impatient to be "on our own," then we may be inclined to have similar attitudes toward those in authority. A great many of us, of course, had mixed feelings about our parents—that is, we were inclined both to be dependent on them and to resent their control. If so, we are likely to have mixed feelings about those who supervise and direct us as adults.

One of the commonest interpersonal problems in modern life is the hostility that develops between parents and children when the latter reach adolescence and maturity. We commented on this relationship earlier but it bears re-examination here because of its relevance to our attitudes toward leaders of the parental type. One of the underlying causes of this hostility is the conflict between parental norms of conduct and peer norms—that is, the difference between what parents want their children to do and what children's friends want them to do. It is very important for the adolescent to maintain the status and acceptance of his friends, but this course of action brings him into inevitable conflicts with the demands of his parents. Another source of difficulty lies in the lack of adequate standards and expectations that adults have for adolescents. We are likely to set conflicting and inconsistent standards and modes of conduct for them. On the one hand, we do not like it when they act without consulting us. We would like to have them learn how to act on their own behalf and develop responsibility but we are unwilling to give them the freedom to develop such independence. It is no wonder that this period of development is marked by frustration, conflict, and hostility!

Since most authority figures we encounter in adult life are likely to be of the parental type (or are viewed by us in that light), and since our most recent experience under the domination and control of our own parents has very likely been tinged with some conflict and frustration, it is easy to understand how our relations with persons who direct and control our actions in adult life should be affected by a carry-over of hostility.

*   *   *

The second type of authority figure is the "manipulator"—the person who creates, accumulates, possesses, uses, and dispenses power by virtue of his ability to analyze persons and situations and to play one individual off against another to good advantage.[1] In the primitive tribe, this kind of person was sometimes represented by the medicine man or witch doctor, or sometimes by one of the wives of the chief who wanted to be sure that her son would obtain precedence over the sons of the other wives. Very often the manipulator does not appear in the open but is a shadowy figure in the background: the power behind the throne, as it were. Very likely he is a person who enjoys power for its own sake—that is, he enjoys controlling persons and situations by exploiting them through their weaknesses. Sometimes he is the politician who gains and exercises his power through election or appointment. Many manipulators are self-seeking individuals, but others appear to be motivated by a genuine desire to improve the welfare of others or of society in general. Their chief characteristic is that they are "lone wolves." Even when they enlist the cooperation and collaboration of others, they are playing their own game and are unhappy unless they are able to exercise or control the power elements inherent in the situation.

The manipulator exercises his power not because he has strength and prestige (like the parental figure) or because he is "better" (like the aristocrat) but because he understands human behavior better than the other members of the organization, more even than the person or persons who are superior in status or authority. However, he has to work through these people because they have the prestige and legitimacy that he lacks. lacks.

In modern times, the manipulative leader may be the self-seeking operator in business, industry, or politics, the person who takes advantage of every angle, every loophole in the law, whose purpose is to built up as much power, economic or political, as possible. At the other extreme of the scale, the manipulative leader is represented by public-spirited persons who are too individualistic to be really democratic and egalitarian, but yet who are lacking in the charismatic, dynamic, and autocratic qualities that go with being a leader of the parental type. People of such varying motivation as Disraeli, Harry Hopkins, Jay Gould, and Otto von Bismarck suggest themselves as examples of the manipulative leader. Many of the business tycoons we referred to in the last chapter could, when necessary, drop their parental roles for the role of the manipulator.

In the developmental sequence that we have been discussing, the manipulative leader represents an advance over the parental type of leader, at least to the extent that he makes an attempt to understand some of the problems of human motivation. The administrator who has no manipulative skill attempts to direct and control his subordinates first through use of his prestige and then, if that fails, through the use of his power. Another way to say this is that he tries to operate by getting his followers to like him and, if that fails, he frightens them into obedience. The manipulator also can be charming or frightening, although he usually avoids extremes of emotional expression. But he has more tools in his kit than charm and threat, for he possesses understanding and superior knowledge about human behavior.

To a large degree, it is the greater understanding and knowledge of the manipulator that makes him so heartily disliked. We are afraid that he knows more about us than is safe or wise for him to know. We feel that we know where we stand with the parental type of leader—after all, he is open and aboveboard. But not so with the manipulative leader. He is the sly and tricky one.

For this reason, manipulative leaders do not like to show themselves in the open, or, if they operate in the open,they try to avoid being identified as leaders of the manipulative type. Hence they go to great lengths—baby kissing, bowling, being photographed milking or pitching hay or riveting—to show that they are one of us. Or, in localities where aristocratic connections count for something, they seek legitimacy by marrying into the "better families" or by having a genealogical study done to show that they are really aristocrats after all.

Manipulative leaders, when they are genuinely interested in public welfare, are very useful people, and much of the important work of the world would go undone if they were eliminated from public life. Because they prefer to work by themselves and dislike to be under the control and supervision of others, we should keep them under careful observation. Otherwise they may involve an entire group or organization in commitments that are beyond the scope of the group or are contrary to its purpose and intent. There is, of course, always the danger of losing control of a group or a program to a manipulative leader who is completely self-centered and who is interested only in exploitation.

*   *   *

We come now to a type of authority figure who is in some ways an extension of the manipulative leader, but who plays a role that is basically different—the expert. The expert becomes a person of power, status, and authority by virtue of his special knowledge, skill and training. He differs from the manipulative leader in that he is not interested in power for its own sake; his chief values in life are not centered around the direction and control of others. His chief interest, rather, is in his speciality, be it law, medicine, education, psychology, chemistry, physics, psychiatry, or whatever. He is drawn into the circle of power because he can help in some special way. The expert is not interested in taking power away from any one or accumulating it for himself, but he is interested in helping those who have the power.

The expert has come into prominence during recent times because of the increasing complexity of civilized existence. There are so many factors that have to be taken into consideration whenever an important move must be made. Running a large manufacturing business calls for specialists in law, labor relations, medicine, psychology, public relations, accounting, economics, and transportation, plus specialists in raw materials and chemical processes. Before the president or the board of directors can change a product or institute a new process, many, if not most, of these specialists must be consulted for their estimation of the probable effect of the proposed change. The president and the board are free agents in the matter. They do not *have* to follow the advice of the experts but the opinion of the latter is likely to carry a great deal of weight. We are somewhat more reluctant to use experts in the field of government, particularly in areas outside the field of physical and biological science. But, in general, there is a slow increase in their status and power even in government circles.

The emergence of the expert has meant that the power of traditional authority figures has been reduced somewhat. Or rather that they have been slowed down or restricted in their use of power. If the person in authority takes the advice of his expert consultants, he has, in effect, given some of his power to them. If he chooses not to take their advice, he has at least postponed his action while consulting with them, and the chances are he will not be as sure of himself as he might otherwise be. In any case, he has acted voluntarily. No one forces him to use the expert; he does so because it is the sensible thing to do.

This new share of power that is being placed in the hands of the expert means that a new avenue to positions of leadership has been opened up. No longer is it necessary to charm or frighten or manipulate people in order to arrive at a position of status and respectability. More and more young people are finding their way into such positions by securing training that will make them experts in one field or another. It is the general public's awareness of the need for trained experts that has helped to keep our college enrollments at world-record heights for the past generation and which today is causing the rapid expansion of graduate schools.

We commented a little earlier on the hostility that is likely to be directed at persons with higher education, so we shall not belabor the subject at this point. However, we cannot help but note that the expert sometimes becomes the target for hostility because of his intellectual honesty, because he cannot and will not say what others want him to say—and because he has little patience with traditional methods. Nevertheless, some experts become so enamored with the power they gain by being consulted that they make *ex cathedra* pronouncements on any and all subjects, regardless of whether they are outside the limits of their competence.

There was once a university town that needed some new schools rather badly. Everyone agreed that the new schools were needed; the only problem was how to finance them. One faction on the school board wanted to finance them on a pay-as-you-go basis by raising the taxes and building one school at a time. They said that it was wasteful to issue bonds because you ended by paying out twice the total expenditure in interest. The other faction admitted that bonding was the more expensive method, but pointed out that the need for schools was urgent, and that it was the better part of wisdom to pay more in the long run but to have the use of the school buildings sooner. The two groups argued and wrangled, as school boards do on occasion, and then one of the members suggested that they consult the expert on municipal finance at the university. Everyone thought this was an excellent idea, and the expert was invited in as a consultant.

And so the school board asked him: "Is is better to operate on a pay-as-you-go basis or is it better to bond?"

The expert thought the matter over carefully, and then he told them the advantages and disadvantages of bonding and the advantages and disadvantages of pay-as-you-go.

The school board said: "Yes, we know. But which one do you recommend?"

The expert shook his head. "You don't understand," he said. "I can explain the advantages and disadvantages of each plan and I can point out some of the risks and difficulties that each entails. But whether you will have your buildings sooner and pay more for them or later and pay less is really up to you."

The school board was very dissatisfied with this advice. They were looking for a nice, clearcut recommendation, preferably one that would satisfy both factions,and here the professor had tossed the problem back in their lap.

The bond faction was a little larger than the other faction, so they pushed a bond issue through and submitted it to the voters. The pay-as-you-go people were hurt and angry. They felt particularly let down by the professor ōf municipal finance because they were sure that he was going to be on the side of economy. So they met in rump session and wondered what they were going to do to stop the rest of the board from carrying through this costly scheme; then someone suggested that they consult Dean Jeffrey. Dean Jeffrey was the head of the medical school and had won international fame as a surgeon. He was easily the most famous man on campus. So the group met with Dean Jeffrey and asked him his opinion of the bond issue. They were delighted when he said that he would give them his strongest support. Which he did. He made speeches, gave out statements to the press, and permitted his name to be used on their campaign literature.

The bond faction was appalled by this maneuver and called it a shocking piece of bad faith, for hadn't the board endorsed the bonds at a formal meeting? They tried to counteract the effects of Dean Jeffrey's activites by having the superintendent of schools make speeches about the urgent need for schools but he was no match for the Dean.

The result was inevitable. The school bonds got only a slight majority, well below the two thirds needed for ratification. The pay-as-you-go people were delighted.

Their joy was short-lived, however. Shortly thereafter they tried to get a pay-as-you-go plan started, and the other members of the board, still smarting from their defeat on the bond issue, voted against the proposal, thus defeating it.

Everyone lost out, especially the school children. Perhaps the moral to this parable is that if you want a good, clearcut, unequivocal opinion from an expert, ask him about a problem outside his own field.

*   *   *

The fourth variety of authority figure we are going to discuss is a newcomer to the field. He is a person that we might call "an artist in human relations."

An artist in human relations is, in the very first instance, a democratic individual. He has deep convictions about the essential equality of all human beings. He respects the right of individuals to make decisions about matters that affect their welfare.

His methods upset parental types of leaders, because they feel that he is not dignified enough, that he lets people take advantage of him, that he lets matters get out of control. They do not like his tendency to share his power with the group. The manipulative leader is not sure whether the artist in human relations is someone who foolishly lets others take advantage of him or whether he is just a very clever manipulator. The experts and consultants vary in their reactions to the artist in human relations. Some of them regard him as an expert in a special field like themselves, others tolerate him, and still others feel that letting people make their own decisions is just compounding ignorance. Many experts are impatient with the artist in human relations because *they* are inclined to depreciate the importance of emotional factors. Such factors are hard to measure and record. It is often difficult to prove that they exist. The experts, being skeptical, brisk, and efficient people, are often inclined to treat problems involving human relations as though they were problems in engineering, physics, or economics. A fellow-psychologist once characterized the over-skeptical expert as a person whose test of reality is the computer—one who says in effect: "If it can't be entered on a punch card, it doesn't exist."

The artist in human relationships is a product of the research and clinical work that has been going on in social psychology, group psychotherapy, education, and sociology during the last generation. This work was pioneered by such people as Kurt Lewin, Ronald Lippitt, Abraham Maslow, and Carl Rogers.[2] We have more to say about the concepts and techniques developed by these workers, but suffice it to say for the present that they have trained and inspired a growing number of leaders in a wide variety of fields who are endeavoring to develop a different kind of leadership, a leadership that grows from and develops the power within the group as opposed to the leadership that tries to keep the group weak and the leader strong.

We have used the word "artist" here because we wish to emphasize the fact that the expert in human relations does not rely on techniques alone. He may use techniques, even novel ones, to achieve his goals, but his greatest strength is his sensitivity to the feelings and needs of the people with whom he works. We would not go so far as to say that this is an inborn talent, for it does appear that people can develop and increase their skill in human relations. Nevertheless, it is basically an artistic ability; it depends on sensitivity and balance and it cannot be attained merely by practising a set of techniques and maneuvers.

Like other leaders, the artist in human relations is not immune from hostility of others. Sometimes it appears because he is just temperamentally unsuited to the kind of group he gets. For example, a sober and studious leader might get a raucuous, noisy group. He might work very hard at being a group leader but not succeed because too large a gap exists between his personality and that of the group. Another kind of leader, equally skilled in human relations, would succeed in the same situation. Another reason for hostility is that some group members are so used to having leaders make the decisions for them that they resist and resent the idea of having to take any responsibility on their own. However, a really skillful artist in human relations should be able to handle this situation successfully, if he has enough time and if influences outside the group are not too strong. As we said earlier, it is when groups are *apathetic*, when they are *passively* hostile, that we have our poorest chances for success.

The field of human relations is so new that much of its lore is still on a tentative basis. We are not sure as yet what it all means, although most of what we have discovered makes better sense and is more workable than the more traditional approaches. The tentative quality of our findings means that we are bound to make some mistakes. This is particularly likely to happen when clearcut decisions have to be made. When a decision has to be made, you act on the basis of the best knowledge and the best guess you can make, and if some of the knowledge has not been tested widely enough, there are bound to be some failures. Some proportion of failures is inevitable, anyway, in human situations because they are so complex. Even the simplest human situation has more complexities than the most complicated machine.

Another source of difficulty and hostility is the tendency of a new field of science to become a cult. "Group dynamics" and "sensitivity training" have become catchwords to the point that some psychologists are reluctant to use the terms lest they be confused with the growing number of "experts," largely self-trained, who are using and misusing the techniques developed by experts in the field of human relations, without being sensitive to the needs of the people they are trying to help. Other workers in the field of group dynamics have been carried away by the idea of developing the power of the group and have forgotten that the individual, too, has some rights.

Because the artist in human relations is a relative newcomer to the field of leadership, it is difficult to appraise his net effect on the relations between authority figures and the people they supervise or guide. There are probably relatively few persons who would qualify as real artists in human relations, although there is a significant number who are in various stages of developing the understanding and skill necessary. One thing is certain, and that is that the field has attracted a great deal of attention, some of it favorable, some not. If this attention does nothing else, it should result in a reappraisal and re-examination of policies and principles that authority figures have been accepting as axiomatic and unchangeable since the beginning of time. Such self-searching is healthy, and if the would-be artist in human relations accomplishes only this, he will have made a sizable contribution.

But those of us who work in the field of human relations think that much more will come of this kind of leadership. We feel, for example, that this kind of leadership will improve mental health, make for happier and more productive employees, and promote better understanding among the citizens of our communities. If so, the present tentative and experimental efforts in this direction deserve much encouragement, for these are advantages and goals well worth the trouble and expense that inevitably accompany the development of a new kind of leadership.

FOOTNOTES CHAPTER 7

[1]The manipulative type of person is also known as "Machiavellian," after Nicolo Machiavelli (1469-1527), whose treatise, *The Prince*, is a masterful compendium of advice for those who would like to acquire power and use it skillfully.

[2]Works by some of these authors will be found listed at the end of this book.

CHAPTER EIGHT

Trademarks of Leadership

Why does a person become a leader? What personality traits, skills, or other characteristics lead us to recognize some people as potential leaders and to ignore or reject others? What is it that makes some people rise to positions of leadership and authority?

These seem like rather basic questions aimed at the essence of leadership. Presumably, if we could ferret out the answers or if we could isolate those special skills or characteristics that make a person a leader, we would know what a nonleader would have to learn in order to become a leader. Yet we know realistically that is isn't that simple.

Leadership is a changing, dynamic thing. The skills and techniques that may work with one group may not work with another. As we pointed out earlier, even the leaders who possess the greatest authority and prestige are not leaders all the time, for there are times when *they* are led, guided, directed, counseled, commanded, or taught. Conversely, virtually all people play leadership roles at various times. The janitor may be at the bottom of the status ladder at the plant, but when he comes home he is a father and a husband. To be sure, his wife may be the dominant one, but *sometimes* he makes suggestions that are followed, *sometimes* he is able to veto a proposal, and *sometimes* he takes the initiative. In a good, friendly discussion, the discussants pass the leadership from one person to another. First, one makes a suggestion, another welcomes it, a third thinks of ways the suggestion might be carried out, and so forth. Leadership is not the sole property of the person at the head of an organization; most of the people in subordinate positions influence others and therefore exercise leadership for the benefit or the detriment of the organization, depending on what they do to expedite or to impede the everyday affairs and the progress of the group.

Some of us exercise leadership more often than others. This is especially true of people who have been appointed to administrative or supervising positions, people who are easily identified by their titles as leaders. However, in any organization there are the unofficial leaders, the ones whose opinions carry a great deal of weight, whose comments can make or break a proposed program of action. Nevertheless, there are certain people who "specialize" in leadership, so to speak, who seek out leadership roles in the groups they enter, and these are the people we are referring to when we speak of leaders in this chapter. What we are principally concerned with here, is not so much what motivates certain people to seek roles as leaders, but *how people behave* when they are in a leadership role, and how the people who play this role most frequently differ from those who play it seldom or in very restricted circumstances like the janitor we just mentioned. However, before we get into the problem of how the behavior of the "habitual leader" tends to differ from that of the "occasional leader," we might at first examine the question of where leadership comes from. Is it a personal attribute of certain people, a special kind of personality, or isn't it?

Probably the most popular theory regarding the development of leadership is that a leader is *a certain kind of person*, one who will rise to the surface in almost any situation. (This is sometimes called the "great man" theory of leadership.) Some psychologists disagree with this theory, maintaining that *situations*, not personalities, determine who shall be the leader. Becoming a leader, they say, is partly accidental, partly a matter of being at the right place at the right time, and partly a matter of having the skills and the talents to supply the kind of leadership needed. They would say, for example, that Napoleon rose to his high position of leadership because the times demanded a leader with his talents. If he had been born fifty or a hundred years earlier, he might have become only a junior officer in some European army instead of a man who changed the face of Europe.

Another theory is that the kind of person who will rise to a position of leadership will depend on the *kind of organization*—that is, certain kinds of organizations produce certain kinds of leaders. A traditional type of organization, made up of people who admire qualities of strength, decisiveness, firmness, and positiveness, will create leaders who display these qualities, whereas a group of professional workers who object to having decisions made for them will get along best with a leader who does not take too much power unto himself, who is willing to give his group maximum freedom. The first group would reject the second kind of leader as too weak, and the second group would reject the first kind of leader as too dictatorial.

There is undoubtedly some validity in all three of these theories or explanations. Very likely there are people who rise to positions of leadership in almost any one of a variety of situations, who adjust and temper their behavior to the emotional climate they encounter. On the other hand, different situations do tend to produce different kinds of leaders. And these leaders in turn must be in tune with the prevailing philosophies that govern the groups they plan to lead, otherwise they will lose their followers and will be supplanted by new leaders of a different sort.

In discussing leadership in this chapter, we are going to assume that there are some qualities of leadership that either are present in people before they become leaders or are developed by them after they have started to function as leaders. We will also assume that much of what we have to say applies to most leaders—leaders in general—regardless of whether they come into leadership by being members of a prominent family, by being placed in a strategic position by some chance or trick of fate, or by having the kind of outlook or personality that is well-attuned to some prevailing philosophy or pattern of belief. And when we talk of leadership, we are thinking principally, although not entirely, in terms of *effective* leadership: leadership which helps the members of a group or organization to meet their individual needs and to achieve the purposes that brought them together.

*   *   *

One of the first requirements of leadership is that it must in some way symbolize the values and purposes of the group or organization. The group must see some relationship, some obvious tie, between themselves and their leaders. For example, school teachers would not be happy serving under a principal or superintendent who has never taught school. He might be a very competent leader and have a good, broad grasp of educational principles, but because he had not "been through the mill," there would always be the feeling that he did not understand the problems of the teacher. Another example: it is very difficult for an individual to be elected to public office in this country unless he has lived in the area or community he is to represent.

If a group feels, rightly or wrongly, that the leader is too different from them, they will feel that he cannot represent them properly, that communication with him will be too difficult. It is all right for the leader to be better than the group members, provided he is better in a way that is approved by the group. This kind of difference can be tolerated, particularly during an emergency. In times of war, or in the period of unrest that follows, a military man looks like a good leader because he exemplifies military virtues. However, in some communities where religious feelings are strong, ministers, priests, and church officials rise to position of high leadership because they are considered to be outstanding in ways that are in keeping with local values. Or a man may become corporation president because he is admittedly a better businessman than the other members of the board of directors. But, on the other hand, groups do not tolerate someone who is better in a way that they do not approve. Louis Koch, the "rate breaker" in Chapter 2 who was given the "silent treatment" by his fellow workers because his production was so much higher than theirs, will not be accepted as a leader if he stays with the Engine Rebuilding Company. His superiority is the kind that makes his fellow workers anxious and hostile. On the other hand, if he excelled in his ability to get grievances settled to the satisfaction of his fellow workers, this kind of superiority might be more easily accepted.

This ability of a leader to assume positive symbolic value for a group is sometimes called "charisma"—a Greek word meaning "favor" or "gift." A charismatic leader is one whose attractiveness has a certain irresistible and inexplicable hold over his followers, who commands loyalty because "he is who he is" and not because of any characteristic that makes sense from a logical or rational point of view. All the great leaders of history had a certain amount of charisma, and it is common to describe a leader whose only appeal appears to have been his symbolic value, rather than his effectiveness as a thinker or planner, as a "charismatic leader." The Ayatollah Khomeini is an example of such a leader, William Jennings Bryan is another, and so is Bonnie Prince Charlie.

Most leaders need a certain degree of charisma to be successful. The keenest mind and the best planner in the group is not likely to be recognized and accepted as a leader unless he is in some way attractive to the group, unless he somehow comes to symbolize what they are looking for in the way of a leader.

Leaders usually differ from others in the amount of interest they develop in the organization and its purposes. This means that a leader is emotionally involved in the group—it becomes a part of him, so to speak. When it prospers, he is happy; when it deteriorates, he is depressed; when the group is criticized, he feels as though the critics were talking about him.

This means also that he cannot have too many conflicting interests because they would interfere with his devotion to the organization. There is a widespread feeling in corporations that an executive must be able to devote a major portion of his concern to the interests of his employer, if he is to be of much value.

The fact that leaders develop strong interest in the group or organization they serve also means that they are less likely to permit personal interests to interfere. If they are to be effective, they cannot afford to build themselves up at the expense of the organization. If this occurs, or even if their subordinates *think* that it is occurring, morale will suffer because they will come to feel that they are being exploited. They will no longer want to do what is required of them because of the feeling that their leaders are taking advantage of them.

One of the ways in which leaders differ most markedly from nonleaders is in their concern about the future. Individual group members differ widely among themselves with regard to their concern about the future of the group, of course, but in general they are less concerned than are their leaders. Group members are more likely to be concerned whether the group is meeting their needs *now* and in the immediate future. Leaders, on the other hand, are more concerned about the long-range plans for the group: how the group may *continue* to meet the needs of its members, how it may meet needs more effectively, how to allow for future difficulties that may keep the group from achieving its purpose, and the like. Leaders are usually more likely to be alert to anticipate events that may threaten the security or the effectiveness of the group or that may be used to the advantage of the group.

Leaders also differ from other people in their drive to get things done—a quality that psychologists call "task orientation.[1]" They appear to derive a certain "normal anxiety" from an unfinished job or an unmet goal that goads them on and on to completion of the task or to some other more or less adequate resolution of the problem. Again, group members vary in their reaction to unfinished tasks, depending on a great many factors, such as the extent to which they are involved in or committed to the fate of the group, the apparent likelihood of success in the task at hand, and their ability to see its relationship to their personal goals. Effective leaders have a real contribution to make here because they are able to see the situation in much broader perspective than the average group member and hence are able to make interpretations that help to encourage others and that involve them more deeply in the work of the group. Because they are concerned with outcomes, they can inspire group members by directing their attention to long-range goals and possibilities and can thus help them sense the importance of the task to be done.

The anxiety of leaders with respect to unfinished work does not mean that they are likely to move impetuously or irrationally. Rather, this is a kind of *normal* anxiety, an anxiety that is related to concern about the welfare of others, about the organization, and about the future. It is the kind of anxiety that produces the hard work, the sustained effort,and the devotion to duty characteristic of effective leaders.

We now come to the use of power, a matter that is very sensitive and that leaders handle in different ways. Sometimes the anxiety felt by a leader about unfinished tasks and the work to be accomplished leads him to use power as a way of achieving the goals of the group. This means, in effect, that he compels group members and subordinates to do the tasks assigned them. Very often this is quite necessary; very often it is the only way that the work will get done, and it may be absolutely essential that the work be done. This may hold true during a time of emergency when certain members of the group are reluctant to take a serious view of crucial problems or issues or pick this time to challenge the right of the leader to lead. Or it may be necessary to use power with people who know only an autocratic kind of leadership and who will not respond to any other kind.

However, power is a dangerous force. It has a fatal attraction. Many a leader has turned to power in times of an emergency and has found it impossible to turn away. For such leaders, one emergency begets another, and life becomes a long series of emergencies that can be met only with the use of power. It is also easy to make the assumption that the people with whom one deals understand power and only power. People who work because they are afraid of their leaders or because they are afraid not to work do not produce very efficiently. They cannot develop their best potentialities. Hence the effective leader in such circumstances tries to find ways whereby power—and, what is equally important, responsibility—can be shared. Those regions of the world where power is closely held by a few leaders are political powderkegs that pose the greatest threat to the international community of nations, whereas those areas where power is most widely distributed are those which are working the hardest to improve the welfare of all humankind. The dangers inherent in monopolizing power apply to both large and small groups, those consisting of hundreds of millions and those consisting of two or three.

The effective leader will therefore be conservative in his use of power and he will bend every effort to bring about its eventual distribution among the members of the group.

Leaders differ from other people in that they are more interested in problems relating to power. Because of the nature of their work, they must continually be concerned about whether they have enough power, whether they are using it wisely, or whether it should be shared more widely. Persons who are on their way to becoming full-fledged leaders. who are practicing their leadership skills, usually engage in activities that are associated with power. They volunteer for committee work, enjoy working with the top leaders of the group, read up on parliamentary procedure, and participate actively in group discussion. Considered as a group, leaders enjoy using power and having the responsibility for groups and organizations.

For the most part, the other members of the group are content to let leaders work with what they consider to be the obnoxious and petty details of the organization, and it is this willingness to sit back and let the leaders and would-be leaders take over that constitutes a real danger. What often happens is that the group as a whole becomes less and less involved in things that really affect them as individuals and as group members, while more and more power becomes concentrated in the hands of a few people. In the end, this works out to the detriment of all concerned. The group members become apathetic and cannot be moved to cooperate or participate or to do their work very effectively. If the group begins to fail in its objectives, members drop out or blame the leaders. At this point they may try to get rid of the leaders or, if circumstances do not permit this, they will sink into deeper apathy or employ some of the maneuvers we described in Chapter 4 as outlets for their hostility.

*   *   *

Much of what we have been talking about—interest in the welfare of the organization, concern for the future, anxiety about tasks that need doing, and the use of power—comes under the heading of *responsibility*.

Leaders differ from other people in their willingness to assume responsibility: to take the initiative, to plan and carry through the tasks that need to be done, to take the credit or the blame, as the case may be.

The willingness to accept responsibility is a key attribute in effective leadership. The world is full of people who are afraid of responsibility, who are made anxious by the merest possibility that responsibility may be theirs. The acceptance of responsibility means acceptance of the possibility of blame for failure. Merely to think of these things causes anxiety for most of us. The acceptance of responsibility also means changing oneself and one's life. Accepting responsibility means some loss of freedom; it means that we can no longer do what we want to do, for we have to do what the job at hand demands.

Most people feel at times that certain important things should be done—someone should see that the beach is cleaned up this year, someone ought to see that we get a new school out this way, someone ought to serve as program committee chairman. But doing these necessary tasks means taking on new responsibilities. The very hint of responsibility arouses anxiety and this in turn immobilizes us. We are frozen into inactivity by the thought of all that may be involved.

It is no wonder, therefore, that effective leaders are in short supply. This is the age of anxiety, and most of us are trying to avoid adding to the anxiety we already have, even if it means that some very important and necessary things go undone. Business, industry, and public affairs are crying for leaders, but anxiety makes cowards of us all—or most of us.

What this means, therefore, is that leaders are somewhat more able to *tolerate* the anxiety that is aroused by responsibility. Undoubtedly they are made anxious by their responsibilities, but they appear to be able to cope with this anxiety better than other people. There are degrees of difference in this among leaders, of course. Some leaders are less able to cope with anxiety, and it makes them petulant, irritable, suspicious, or lacking in firmness—whatever their characteristic way of dealing with anxiety happens to be. Even the grim, hard-boiled leader is very likely a victim of this kind of anxiety. Being hard-boiled and inconsiderate is a common way of hiding anxiety from oneself and others.

So far we have said two things about leadership and anxiety. We have said that leaders are more inclined to develop the *normal* anxiety that goes with being concerned about the future and with wanting to tackle and finish jobs that have to be done, and we have said that they are better able to tolerate the anxiety that comes with the assumption of responsibility. But there are even more ways that leadership touches upon anxiety. Even while they are coping with their *own* anxiety, people who are effective leaders show a marked ability to allay the anxieties of subordinates or group members. That is, they are able to allay the *neurotic* anxieties of group members, the anxieties that make groups ineffective, needlessly hostile, and easily distracted from their main goals.

We all know the role of the anxiety-reducer. It is a traditional role for leaders to play—to remain calm and reassuring while everything is in a turmoil and panic is in the air. It is in some ways a parental role. When we were children and were convinced that there was a bogey in the basement, it was our parents who reassured us, who told us that there really weren't any bogies and then went down into the basement with us to prove it. And even as adults we have not entirely outgrown childish patterns and hence need this kind of reassurance occasionally from our leaders, particularly in time of crisis.

However, what is not often recognized is that leaders have a counter-responsibility to *arouse* normal anxiety at times. (We mentioned this in Chapter 5 when we were discussing the role of the leader as an interpreter.) There are times when we are too complacent, when we knowingly or unknowingly plod along in our accustomed ways, unmindful of hidden dangers, of weak spots on our economy or our moral fiber, of wrongs to be righted, or of important work undone. Leaders tend to be persons who can interpret our situation to us, who can present us with the facts that we should know and are trying to overlook, and who will goad us a little to carry through the work that must be done. This is a difficult task for leaders to accomplish because, as we indicated earlier, we are all trying to *avoid* anxiety, and the leader who makes us uncomfortable by arousing it—even normal anxiety—runs the risk of unpopularity. And the unpopular leader, the leader who has no followers, is no longer a leader.

Because of the risks involved in arousing anxieties, many otherwise effective leaders let this part of their responsibility go by default. And who can blame them? Hence, most of the anxiety-provoking that goes on in public life is done by persons who do not have much following as leaders and have little to lose thereby. Sometimes their criticisms are disturbing enough to attract attention, with the result that they assemble a following and become leaders in their own right. Very often such people become tagged with the label of "alarmist" or "extremist" or "activist." Undoubtedly many who are so labelled are emotionally disturbed people, but some of them actually can understand the meaning of things more clearly than most of us. It is difficult or perhaps impossible to tell which of these disturbing people are true and which are false prophets. Perhaps we can only wait and see. However, we should note that the founders of many of the world's religious sects as well as many early scientists were regarded by the people of their day as misfits, visionaries, and heretics.

*   *   *

Leaders tend to possess a high degree of what psychologists call "frustration tolerance"—the ability to go ahead in spite of repeated failures and not be unduly disturbed by them. Effective leaders are more likely to accept the possibility of failure, to be aware that everything one undertakes carries within it the seeds of failure, and not to think of themselves as special persons who the gods have shielded from failure forever more.

Because leaders are more inclined to accept the possibility of failure, they are also more likely to have taken precautions and to have laid alternate plans for action. They are less inclined to be thrown into a panic or become deeply dismayed. This does not mean that even effective leaders are paragons or saints. When they fail they are likely to be irritated or momentarily depressed—after all, they are human—but their recovery tends to be rapid and they are inclined to follow each failure by a renewed attack on the main problem. Because they are more dedicated to the welfare of the organization, they are less prone to let failure or frustration impede their progress more than momentarily.

Frustration and hostility go hand in hand. Hostility is frequently the result of frustration, and the leader sees them as two of his chief hazards. If he fails too many times, this may arouse the hostility of the group and lead to the end of him as a leader. Or he may turn his hostility on himself, on the group, or on outside forces. Perhaps the hostility will be richly deserved and long overdue, perhaps not. Perhaps it might even be helpful and will clear the air for a while. But hostile behavior cannot be continued for too long a time. The chronically hostile leader is an ineffective leader, since he is too distracted from his main task to be able to further the best interests of his group or of mankind in general.

Most of the hostility with which the leader must deal comes from the people he supervises, directs, guides, and assists—from the "consumers" of his leadership. Leaders in general show a greater ability to tolerate this hostility than do non-leaders. As we stated previously, hostility is likely to arouse anxiety. Either leaders are able to cope with this kind of anxiety better than most people, or else being on the receiving end of hostility does not seem to get under their skin as much as it does with people who are not leaders. Some leaders develop this "coping ability" at an early age. Others are quite sensitive to hostility until they get to be leaders and then, over a period of years, learn to bear it more easily. During the first years of leadership, most of us are likely to be oversensitive and overanxious, and the hostility that is the inevitable lot of the leader cuts more deeply. But after a few years, we become more sure of ourselves, particularly if we can learn that these hostile gestures are, for the most part, not the result of any personal defect but are part of being a leader.

Undoubtedly some of our reluctance to assume the responsibility that goes with being a leader is related in some way to our awareness that being a leader means becoming the target for hostility, and this awareness, too, arouses some anxiety. And so most of us conclude that it is "safer" to be a follower than a leader. When it comes to hostility, it is much easier to give than to receive.

*   *   *

Leaders not only have a greater tolerance for hostility than do people who are not leaders, but they also have a greater tolerance for isolation—

the feeling of being separated from the rest of the group. Although we have gone a long way from the days when the captain of a vessel was expected to take his meals alone in his cabin, there is nevertheless a feeling of a separation and difference that underlies the relationships of leaders and the other members of the group or organization. Sometimes leaders can minimize this isolation by insisting that they be called by their first names and by going to great lengths to "fraternize" with their subordinates but they never get rid of it altogether. Most leaders come to accept it as one of the inevitable results of becoming a leader. Some regret it and try to eliminate it or make amends, as we have indicated, whereas others seem to enjoy it.

Fred E. Fiedler of the University of Washington in Seattle has conducted extensive studies of the relationship between leaders and members of task groups—that is, groups having specific goals, as contrasted with informal social groups. The task groups he observed consisted of basketball teams, Air Force bomber crews, sales staffs of farm supply cooperatives, surveying teams, Army tank crews, and workers operating open-hearth furnaces in steel mills. When Fiedler examined the performance of the groups, he found more psychological "distance" between members of the more-successful groups and their supervisors, as compared to the relations between supervisors and group members of less-successful groups. In other words, supervisors in the more-successful groups were more aloof, cool, and distant than the supervisors of less successful groups. The supervisors of the less-successful groups apparently felt it necessary to socialize with the people they supervised and worked harder to be liked. This made it more difficult for them to make demands on their people and to exact penalties when performance goals were not met.

It is very likely that a great many people become leaders partly because they *do* feel themselves to be different somehow from the other members of the group. For them, becoming a leader is one way of expressing that difference. The aristocrat, the authoritarian, and the parental type of leader take this isolation as a matter of course. The manipulative leader may not accept it as readily, although much of his behavior is directed at emphasizing the differences between himself and the rest of the group. The expert is still less concerned about maintaining a discreet distance between himself and others, although he is constantly being reminded of the reality of his isolation when he attempts to communicate. It is difficult to translate technical knowledge and concepts into lay language. Many experts do not even try to find better ways of communication and fall back on an autocratic solution of the dilemma—they insist that others take their orders or recommendations at face value and not question the reasons why.

The artist in human relations is made more anxious by his isolation as a leader than is any of the other types of leaders. If he is really effective, he will not attempt to pretend that group members do not feel a difference between themselves and leaders. Instead, he accepts the existence of such feelings and tries to counteract them by attempting to involve the members of the organization or group in the practice of leadership—in making policy, for example. However, the feeling of difference and isolation has deep traditional and psychological roots, roots that are not easily eradicated.

                    *   *   *

Another attribute that is characteristic of leaders is their ability to communicate. Skill in communication is basic to the interpretative function of leadership that we mentioned earlier. Leaders, taken as a whole, are more able to put their ideas into words. One way to get a rough measure of the leadership potential in a group of people who have been brought together for the first time is to note the kind and the amount of talking they do. Those who speak up the oftenest, who make the most contributions to the conversation, are more likely to turn out to be the leaders of the group if it continues to work together.[2] Those who do not talk at all are almost certain not to become leaders, unless leadership happens to be something that the members of the group are trying to avoid.

The process of communication involves some very complex skills, and it is a subject that we want to explore more fully in the chapters to come. Hence we shall merely mention it here as one of the several ways that leaders distinguish themselves from other people.

What we have tried to do in this chapter is to cover some of the most important differences between people who are leaders and people who are not leaders. In doing so, we have had to make some generalizations and have had to overlook a lot of differences between the various kinds of leaders. Furthermore, each leader plays his role and organizes his behavior differently from any other leader. Nevertheless, people who play leadership roles in life—particularly those who play them most often—do display all or most of the characteristics we have mentioned. They *are* more deeply involved in the group or organization than most of the other members, they *are* more concerned with power, they *do* seem to have greater stamina or ability to tolerate unpleasant feelings, and they *are* superior in their ability to communicate. And does this imply the persons who display these qualities are potential leaders? Very likely they are, particularly if they symbolize or represent the values that the group holds to be important, values that are related to the basic purposes of the group.

FOOTNOTES CHAPTER 8

[1]See B.M. Bass and G.H. Dunteman, Behavior in groups as a function of self-interaction, and task orientation, *Journal of Abnormal and Social Psychology*, 1963, vol. 66, pp. 419-428.

[2]See R.M. Sorrentino and R.G. Boutillier, The effect of quantity and quality of verbal interaction on ratings of leadership ability, *Journal of Experimental Social Psychology*, 1975, vol. 11, pp. 403-411; and G. Gintner and S. Lindskold, Rate of participation and expertise as factors in influencing leader choice, *Journal of Personality and Social Psychology*, 1975, vol. 32, pp. 1085-1089.

CHAPTER NINE

Effective Leadership Means
Effective Communication

From the viewpoint of the consumer of leadership, the essence of leadership is contained in *what* the leader communicates and *how* he communicates it.

This means that persons who want to become leaders must learn to communicate effectively, and it means that leaders who want to improve their effectiveness must improve their communication.

This looks like a relatively simple prescription. It is—deceptively simple. At first blush it looks as though we have said that learning to lead means learning to write and speak more clearly. This is a common interpretation of the word "communication." But if we limit communication to this interpretation, we commit a double error.

The first error lies in assuming that communication is, essentially, telling others what we mean, think, or feel. Communication certainly does involve self-expression, but it also involves being able to understand what *others* mean, what *they* think or feel. It is interesting that in our schools we lay great stress and spend much time on the skills of self-expression. We spend some time on teaching people to read, too, but the amount of time we invest in teaching this skill grows smaller each year as students go up the educational ladder. And very little time, if any, is spent in teaching people how to *listen*.

Our neglect of listening as a field of education is related to the second error we commonly commit in thinking about communication, and that is to regard communication as something that can be separated from the rest of life or something that can easily be split up into distinct skills and techniques. To be sure, we can make such separations *in our mind*, if we have some special objective like that of practising a specific communicative skill, but what we usually forget is that these distinctions exist *only in our minds*. For the truth of the matter is that communication is part of anything and everything we do that involves other people directly or indirectly. It is even impossible for us to walk through a room containing other people without communicating something about ourselves—how we feel about things in general and how we feel about the people in the room. Let us look at some people who are communicating in this way, as seen through the eyes of the office receptionist.

Myra didn't like the part of her job that required her to be at her post five minutes before the office opened. If there was anything she could use in the morning, it was five minutes more sleep. But the thing she did like was to watch people come in. Being there five minutes early gave her a kind of advantage over the other people in the office. For one thing, she could "kind of tell" what people were really like—before they got their "office face" on for the day.

Like Kay Fletcher, the general manager's secretary. During the day she was always pleasant and obliging, efficient but helpful, even with the other girls. But when she came through the front door at 8:25, she looked intense and grim as if it would hurt her to smile.

Of course, other people looked about the same when they came in as they were all day. Old Mr. Wagner would come in mincing and smirking. He always wore the latest in name-brand ties and shoes and made sure that all the women in the office knew that he had an "open marriage." Myra had him spotted the first day she saw him walk in.

You could tell which office boys were going to stay with the firm and work up through the ranks by the way they walked in. The ones who were going to stay looked and acted more serious. Something about them said that they were the kind who played for keeps. Even when they joked with you, you knew they could be serious the next minute. Of course, some of them fooled you. Art Little didn't have a serious bone in his body when he first came to work. But after he had a couple of brushes with Mr. Nelson, the assistant manager, he quieted down. Six months later he wasn't even walking and talking like the same person. Myra was glad that he stayed on, but she "sort of preferred" him the way he used to be.

You could tell that Ken Van Damm was the top salesman in the office. When he came in you could see that he was a man with a lot of energy. Even when he was tired he had a lot of energy. There was a kind of restlessness to him even when he was standing around talking to the fellows near the drinking fountain.

As people come in the door and go past Myra's desk, their "body language" tells something about them—little revealing glimpses of who they really are and who they think they are.

*   *   *

The big problem in communication is not that of making certain that we are communicating, for we are communicating *something* whenever we are with others, but rather one of helping others to understand us better and understanding them better at the same time. We cannot be concerned with one of these skills to the exclusion of the other.

Dr. Winkler looked up as William Helmuth entered the office. He motioned for him to sit down and then wrote for a minute, jotting down notes on his last patient. He then turned in his swivel chair so that he was facing Mr. Helmuth.

Mr. Helmuth smiled in a faltering, embarrassed sort of way.

"I'm awful sorry I'm late, Doctor," he said. "I was just getting ready to come here when the boss called me into his office. And then when I got there, he got a couple of long phone calls, and I finally had to leave without talking to him. I'm kind of worried about it, because business hasn't been so good, and I've lost so much time during the last two months. . . ."

Dr. Winkler broke in on what he was afraid was going to be a long recital of woes and said:

"Well, I'm glad that you came in, William, even if it was late, because I have some good news for you. The tests show pretty definitely that there's nothing much wrong with your lungs. In fact, except for that wheezy cough of yours, you're in pretty good shape."

Mr. Helmuth smiled again, rather wanly.

"I'm sure glad to hear that," he said. "I don't think I could handle a fancy operation right now. If I get fired or laid off. . . ."

"But I am concerned about that cough of yours," Dr. Winkler went on, briskly. "It seems to me that there must be some asthmatic involvement. I suggested that when you first came to see me, if you remember. I think you ought to see an allergist about it. Dr. Consol has an office on the seventh floor—I think it's Room 716—and has been able to help quite a few patients of mine. If you like, I can send him a report of our findings here."

He paused, waiting for some indication or reaction from Mr. Helmuth. But Mr. Helmuth said nothing. He was looking up at the ceiling with his eyes half shut. His mouth was pursed and he was rubbing his lower lip, thoughtfully. Dr. Winkler waited a bit and then said with a note of irritation in his voice:

"Well, William, would you like me to refer you to Dr. Consol?"

Mr. Helmuth shuddered slightly and then looked at the doctor.

"I guess I was thinking about my job," he murmured. "No, Doctor, I guess I better talk it over with the wife first before I see another doctor." He laughed, humorlessly. "You know we don't have any health insurance, and we got to figure how to pay your bill first before we go running up any others."

"Just as you say, William," said Dr. Winkler. There was a note of disappointment in his voice. One of the hardest things in the world was to get patients to do things that were in their own interest. Sometimes it looked as though they actually didn't want to get well.

"When you decide you're ready to see Dr. Consol, I'll send the report over." And he thought to himself as Mr. Helmuth left the room, "Ten to one he never goes."

To be sure, Dr. Winkler is a busy man. He couldn't begin to give adequate service to the patients who clog his waiting room if he stopped and listened to all the problems of all his patients. Perhaps Dr. Winkler is trying to help too many patients or perhaps the answer is that Mr. Helmuth should be seeing a clergyman or a social worker or a psychologist—someone besides a busy doctor who has patients with symptoms which are far more serious than Mr. Helmuth's.

Whatever the best solution is, it is plain that neither Mr. Helmuth nor Dr. Winkler are communicating very effectively with each other. It is hard for Mr. Helmuth to give his full attention to the doctor, because he is worried about losing his job. He is literally tied into a knot of anxiety and needs to get his troubles off his chest before he can be receptive to communication on any other subject. Dr. Winkler does not realize how disturbed his patient is. He sees Mr. Helmuth as a man who has come to see him about a wheezy cough and he cannot understand why his advice is not taken, much less listened to. However, he has come to accept the fact that many patients who come to see him do not seem to be interested in the advice they are paying for and he has become a little cynical. He used to worry about such things and would go to great lengths to try to explain to his patients exactly what was involved and why it was wise to follow his advice, but he no longer goes to such trouble. He has given up trying.

One of Dr. Winkler's difficulties is that he has fallen into the trap that awaits us all, that of assuming that communication is a problem of getting your points over, getting the other person to understand. He does not see how communication is a simultaneous problem in understanding and being understood. Perhaps if he had listened to Mr. Helmuth sympathetically for a few minutes, or if he had requested Mr. Helmuth to come back at a time when he was less upset, the chances for communication would have been much better.

What we are saying, of course, is that communication has to be two-way if it is to work. In the situation we just described, Dr. Winkler is trying to tell Mr. Helmuth what he should do about his cough, and Mr. Helmuth is trying to tell Dr. Winkler how upset he is about his job. This is typical of what happens when people try to maintain communication on a one-way basis.

We are somewhat inclined to put the largest measure of responsibility for placing communication on a two-way basis on the shoulders of Dr. Winkler, just as we shall be saying throughout this book that leaders can do more about making communication effective than nonleaders. They have greater power and more freedom to bring about changes in interpersonal relationships, others defer to their initiative, and they are the ones who set the tone. We shall have more to say about this later when we discuss leaders and their effect on emotional climate, but first we want to say something more about the reasons why people have difficulty in communicating.

Making communication a two-way process is more than merely opening up avenues or channels. Some people in management circles see two-way communication as a matter of having suggestion boxes or of holding meetings of all the employees. Mass meetings can sometimes be used for certain communicative purposes to good advantage, but they can also be worse than ineffectual. Some of them are reminiscent of the mess sergeant who suddenly appeared at the head of a table in the mess hall with blood in his eye and a meathook in his hand.

"I hear that some of the guys don't like the food," he growled. "I'd like to know who they are and what it is they don't like. Speak up, go ahead, I'm waiting."

The silence that followed was deafening.

*   *   *

Making two-way communication work means that a number of conditions have to be met.

In the first place, the leaders must have a sincere desire to understand what their subordinates have to say. This means that they believe that what subordinates have to say is important, that it is worthwhile listening to.

This is a difficult condition for leaders to meet, generally speaking, because it goes against so much that is traditional in leadership. If the leader tends to be somewhat parental (and most of us who are leaders *are* somewhat on the parental order), admitting that our subordinates may have ideas that are as good as ours is very much like parents admitting that children are capable of having workable ideas on running a family. This may be an unfair comparison, because our adult subordinates and group members are not children. (We shall ignore, for the time being, the strong probability that children *can* participate in making plans and decisions that affect them, particularly in their more mature years.) What we are describing here is how leaders *feel*. We are not saying that subordinates think like children, but we are saying that leaders often *act* as though subordinates think like children. Incidentally, when leaders expect subordinates to think and behave like children and are successful in conveying this idea to them, what often happens is that subordinates *do* think and behave like children. There are, basically, two kinds of childish ways for subordinates to behave—they can become dependent, passive, unable to think for themselves or they can become rebellious and destructive. In other words, the reaction to such treatment sometimes goes to extremes of passive or active hostility.

Inasmuch as almost any important move that leaders may undertake in order to change the relationship between themselves and their subordinates will be regarded by the latter with some suspicion, leaders who are attempting to improve communication by putting it on a two-way basis should be prepared for suspiciousness, lack of cooperation, and even resentment. Until subordinates have had a chance to try the newer methods and see that they work, they will be wondering what their leaders have up their sleeves.

A second condition that must be met if leaders are to put communication on a two-way basis is that they must be aware of some of the difficulties inherent in turning ideas and feelings into words.

In an article published in *Fortune* some years ago and addressed to college students, Peter F. Drucker made the point that the ability to organize and express ideas effectively in speaking and writing is the *key* skill that can and should be learned in college. He even went so far as to recommend that students who hope to advance in business and industry take courses in poetry and short-story writing. He did not, of course, expect that many students would become poets or short-story writers, but he had found that these courses help one develop economy and style in self-expression.

Economy in self-expression is an especially valuable skill. Many people—even leaders—communicate poorly because they talk all around their subjects and say what they have to say several times. As they flounder around in a veritable sea of verbiage, they realize that they are not communicating very well and that their audiences are becoming bored and hostile. The more they realize that they are "losing their audience," the more anxious they become, and the more anxious they become, the more they talk.

The writing of manuals, announcements, memos and other communications media is another activity where leaders encounter difficulty. Some have tried to use readability measures like the Flesch formula as a way of bringing the language of printed communications down from the heights of technical abstraction, or from the depths of bureaucratic gobbledygook, to the level of the common man. While these attempts have undoubtedly helped to some degree, they have not always improved communication of ideas and feelings. Very often, the application of formulas has taken the color out of what has been written, resulting in a flat and insipid text. Written and printed communication should not only hold the interest of the reader, but should also convey *feeling*. For example, in an organization where management is making a sincere attempt to share its power and to enlist employees as collaborators in the general productive effort, written and printed communication must convey the *feeling* of this desire to include employees as "partners in production." In another kind of organization—the military, for example—where, it is argued, collaboration with subordinates on an equal basis is neither practical nor desirable, written and printed communication needs to carry the ring of authority without humiliating or infuriating those to whom it is addressed.

People who have learned how to be really effective communicators have developed skills that go far beyond the ability to manipulate words. They have developed a faculty, skill, or sensitivity that psychologists call *empathy*. We mentioned empathy previously when we discussed a baby's ability to sense his mother's moods and feelings. When we talk about leaders being empathic, we are, of course, using it in a much broader sense. A leader has to be empathic because he has to know how his attempts to express himself are being received. Is he achieving the desired effect? If not, is it because he is using language that group members and subordinates do not understand? Or is it because he is describing a concept that is completely different from anything they have experienced? Or is his audience understanding him in *spite* of what he says—that is, is he revealing feelings that he is trying to conceal from others as well as from himself?

A leader learns how his audience ("audience" is used in the broad sense here, meaning any person or group to whom one attempts to communicate) reacts and feels by watching the expressions on their faces, by noting what they do (or don't do) as they listen to him or read his communication , and by listening to their tones of expression and gestures while they talk. He tries to spend as much time as possible in listening, for it is through listening to people with as much sensitivity and perception as one can muster that one gains an understanding of the ways in which they see things, the frames of reference into which they fit all that they hear and see.

A leader who has learned to be empathic is able to fit himself into the mood and outlook of those with whom he communicates. In effect, he is able to put himself into their shoes and listen to himself as he sounds. When he writes up an announcement of change in procedure for his manufacturing plant, he is careful to show how it will affect wages and jobs. He does this because he knows that the first thing that comes to the mind of an employee when he hears about a change is "How will it affect me?" and he asks himself continually "If I were a worker, how would this sound to me? What would I look for?"

The clergyman in delivering his sermon thinks, "How far can I push the congregation on this issue? I want to stir them up, maybe make them a little angry, but I don't want to get them too upset, too disturbed." So he depends on his empathic understanding of the congregation to guide him.

If Dr. Winkler, who figured in the anecdote at the start of this chapter, had been more empathic, he would have been aware that Mr. Helmuth was too anxious to be interested in finding out why he had a wheezy cough, and perhaps he would have sensed that patients who are expected to call him "Dr. Winkler" do not necessarily like to be addressed by their first names.

Empathy can be learned, if we are willing to believe that what other people think and feel is important and worth knowing. It can be learned by listening to people in a different way—not so much to *what they are saying* but *how* they are saying it. And above all, one listens to find out *what people mean.*

People don't always mean what they say. Or, more likely, people mean a great deal more than they say. "I love you" can mean "I *think* I love you," or "I think you *want* me to say I love you," or "I know this sounds silly but I *do* love you," or any one of an infinite number of things, depending on how it is said, the conditions under which it is said, who is saying it, and who is listening. Anything that is said or done occurs against a shifting background of events and conditions. It is these events and conditions that give words and deeds much of their meaning, and empathy in its broadest sense embraces the understanding of the events and conditions into which the word or deed will be launched. This means knowing the audience—their values, beliefs, prejudices, and interests—and it means knowing what conditions will exist or what happenings will be likely to occur that will influence the audience's understanding.

It takes a great deal of patience and a great deal of trial-and-error experience to become empathic. People who work in a face-to-face relationship—doctors, lawyers, social workers, priests, psychologists, to name a few—usually learn to develop empathy as part of their professional skill. Other kinds of leaders develop this ability, too, although one gets the impression that there is a great deal of variation. It is very likely that when leadership fails—when leaders no longer lead—it is at least partly because the people in power lack sufficient empathy.

One of the difficulties about empathy is that it cannot be very easily measured or recorded on an IBM card or fed into a computer. In this it resembles a lot of other human skills and qualities that provide the social lubrication and the basic motivation needed to make collaboration and cooperation possible. Because empathy has to do with feelings and emotions, perhaps many are inclined to discount it, to deny its importance, or perhaps even to doubt its existence. Yet there is plenty of evidence, if we want to look for it, that when leaders work within a framework of human values, the organizations and groups they supervise not only provide more satisfying experience for participants, but are actually more efficient, effective, and productive.

*   *   *

As we said earlier, we are much too inclined to look at communication as a process of telling somebody something. Even when we endorse the idea of two-way communication, it still appears as a to-and-from business—the leader over here and the audience over there, and communication as something that goes on back and forth between them. However, what we have been trying to suggest in this chapter is that communication be thought of as doing something *with* an audience. Communicating *with* someone implies mutual confidence and understanding. Above all, it implies empathy, for without empathy, there is very little understanding.

Becoming empathic and communicating *with* others means that the leader will give up some of his isolation, for if he is a successful communicator, he will draw psychologically closer to the other members of the group or organization. His dependence on power and authority will decrease, and his dependence on understanding and acceptance will increase. Probably he never will give up *all* of his isolation, because, as long as he plays a leadership role, he has different interests and a broader responsibility than the other members of the group or organization.

Some leaders will be unable to make the transition because of the inability to convince other key persons in the group or organization of the need for such a change, because the structure and traditions of the group do not permit such a relationship, or because they do not have a personality that is appropriate to such a relationship. Very often all three of these conditions operate simultaneously. Leaders and organizations have to decide for themselves how important it is for them to preserve the status quo—to keep the lines of authority and the power-relationships just as they are. Sometimes instituting changes stirs up so much anxiety and disturbance that it seems desirable to leave things as they are, even though the proposed changes would lead to improved communications, greater efficiency, higher production, and greater satisfaction and happiness in the long run. The story of Sam Raton and the Smith River Furniture Company is an example of what happens when feelings and anxieties are aroused by the threat of change.

The Smith River Furniture Company was a medium-size factory situated in a small town in the mountains about a hundred miles from a large city. At one time it produced a diversified line, but during recent years it has specialized for the most part in unpainted furniture to meet the growing paint-it-yourself trade. The company produced modest but steady profits for its owners. The wages it paid were not as high as those paid in the larger cities and towns of the state.

Owners and employees more or less accepted the company as it was, but an outside observer would probably notice a number of factors that could stand study. For one thing, employment was not very steady. There were slack seasons that lasted for weeks when the plant was shut down completely. Then there were times when it operated on a three-day week. There were also times when the plant operated two shifts a day and Saturdays, with overtime. Labor turnover was high among the unskilled and semiskilled workers. The age of the skilled employees increased year by year, for very few of the local youth seemed interested in the apprenticeship program offered by the company.

Sam Raton came to work for the company as its personnel manager when it was decided to combine such functions as personnel records, training, safety, and employee morale under one department. Sam was a local boy who had gone to the state university. He taught a couple of years and then went back to do some graduate work in psychology. Like most local boys, he had worked in the furniture plant during summer vacations. Even during these brief periods of employment, Sam had impressed the management as a particularly willing and conscientious worker.

When Sam first came to work as a personnel manager, the other members of the managerial staff greeted him cordially enough, but he soon found that he was at the bottom of the totem pole as far as status was concerned. One day, when he had been on the job a month, he came back to his office from a safety survey to find both of his clerks typing addresses on envelopes. Just then the advertising manager strolled in.

"I'm glad I found you, Sam," he said carelessly. "I was asking Mr. Bidwell where I could get someone to address and stuff envelopes to send out these circulars and he said I could use your staff. Hope you didn't have anything too important for them to do."

Sam kept his own personnel records for the next two days.

Everywhere Sam went in the plant, he found evidence of inefficiency and waste. True, most of it was minor, although some of the things he saw cost the company thousands of dollars. For example, there was the time someone sent an order to Portland, Maine, instead of Portland, Oregon. To be sure, there is some inefficiency and waste in every organization of any size but what concerned Sam was that no one seemed to care.

As Sam talked to the young people who were hired to fill the unskilled jobs in the plant and who quit a few months later, he found an undercurrent of dissatisfaction and hostility. They did not like to work with the older men in the plant. They felt they shouldn't have to put up with being criticized at every turn, with getting stuck with the dirtier jobs. They felt that the foreman and the older woodworkers had it in for them and for their part they were happy to leave.

Sam was disturbed by this situation. One of the things that Mr. Bidwell, the general manager, had asked him to give special attention to was employee turnover. After a few weeks, he tried to spend some time each day talking with the foremen to see whether anything could be done to reduce the turnover. He found only two that were interested in talking about the subject. The others acted as though he were suggesting that they coddle their employees and told him that if he would do *his* job and find them people who were interested in working instead of sitting around batting the breeze, the turnover problem would solve itself. Sam had no answer for than one except to say that he was doing all he could to recruit new hands.

Sam decided to spend most of his time with the two foremen who *were* interested in reducing turnover and he worked out a plan whereby each employee hired in their departments would come back to him once a week for the first month for a twenty-minute interview. During that time the worker was free to talk about anything he or she wished and was assured that anything said would be kept in confidence. If the employee brought up complaints about the company or about the work, Sam asked if it would be all right to discuss the problem with the foreman, promising not to reveal the name of the person making the complaint. Sometimes the worker would give permission and sometimes not. Sam made it a practice to have lunch with the two foremen twice a week and would go over the problems he had collected. If there were no problems, they just talked about whatever came to mind.

The result was that turnover in the two departments concerned dropped away to almost nothing. Furthermore, in his trips around the plant, Sam noticed that matters were going better in the two departments than elsewhere in the plant. Their working space was neater, there were fewer accident hazards, and the workers seemed more interested in their work. Absenteeism was lower, too. He was quite pleased with what he had done, but he was still disturbed about the fact that the other departments had so far resisted his attempts to work more closely with them.

After Sam had been on the job some ten months, he decided that it was time to expand the scope of his operations, so he prepared a special report for Mr. Bidwell, explaining what he was doing with the two departments and what the results had been. He avoided any mention of lack of cooperation on the part of the other foremen. He also avoided making any specific proposals as to how personnel practices might be improved in other departments, but he did conclude by saying that he wanted to talk to Mr. Bidwell about ways to reduce turnover and absenteeism for other departments. He was not sure where he stood with Mr. Bidwell, and he thought it best to let Mr. Bidwell take the initiative when it came to ways and means—unless, of course, Mr. Bidwell invited his suggestions.

He sent the report in and made an appointment to see Mr. Bidwell a few days later, to give him time to read the report and digest its contents.

When he walked into Mr. Bidwell's office on the appointed day, the latter was affable and friendly. He offered Sam a chair and a cup of coffee and then took out Sam's report from its folder.

"That's quite a job of work you have done there, Sam," he said. "That's what I like about you college-trained fellows. You know how to write a report that's worth reading. When I first took this job, I tried to get written reports every week out of the foremen, but do you think I could do it? No, sir. After I read the first few sad specimens, I knew I was licked, so we worked out a set of forms for them to put in numbers and make checks. We're still using them. Pretty good forms, don't you think? Gives you a bird's-eye view of production for the week at a glance."

He waved a sheaf of forms at Sam.

Sam said he thought they were well-thought-out, too, although his private feeling was that they ought to be supplemented by other means of communication, and he wondered whether Mr. Bidwell *really* knew what went on in the plant.

"Yes," Mr. Bidwell continued, "I think we have a real find in you, Sam.

How would you like to write all our reports? We have the accounting department to do all the figures, of course, but I mean the descriptive part. It would amount to about a dozen a year."

Sam cleared his throat. "I'm certainly glad to know that you think I write a good report," he said, "and I think that I could help out with some of the other reports that have to be done. But I was wondering whether you had a chance to go over the part where I mentioned turnover and absenteeism?"

Mr. Bidwell frowned.

"I was hoping you wouldn't bring that up, Sam," he said. "I was really hoping you'd let that plan of yours drop. You don't know it, boy, but I've *really* had to go to bat for you during the last month, and I don't know how much longer I can do it. The wolves are really howling for your scalp, Sam."

"But I don't understand," Sam stammered. "You *asked* me to cut down on absenteeism and turnover. That's why you hired me."

"Yes, I know," Mr. Bidwell told him, "but I had no idea you were going to pull some trick that would turn the plant inside out. For the last six weeks, I have been getting complaints every two or three days. At least three foremen have asked me personally to get rid of you. That's why I was glad you came in to see me because I wanted a chance to talk to you about it."

Sam knit his brows in perplexity. "What are they complaining about?" he asked. "And why didn't they come to me?"

"It's hard to say, really," Mr. Bidwell said, thoughtfully. "It seems mostly that you are making it difficult for them to deal with their men. They say that there is a lot more backtalk and loafing since you have come here. And a couple of them pointed out to me that the absenteeism rate and the rate of turnover have gone up in their departments. And at least three of them have said that you refused to cooperate with them. I guess that's the sum of it."

Sam was aghast. "Why, *they're* the ones who refused to work with me when I was trying out this plan that cut down absenteeism and turnover. How can they accuse *me* of not being cooperative?"

"Well, the fact remains that they have," replied Mr. Bidwell, "and I am forced to point out that as a staff member you are not a part of the operating force of this concern. In other words, if you like it straight from the shoulder, it's up to *you* to cooperate with *them*. Whatever happens, production must not suffer. We can't afford to take chances, you know."

Sam made one last attempt. "Mr. Bidwell, I think I could reduce turnover and absenteeism and improve production in every department, if you'd give me a free hand. I've proven that it can be done in two departments. If it will work for them, it will work for the whole plant."

Mr. Bidwell pulled his chair closer to Sam, put his hand on Sam's knee, and looked at him earnestly.

"Nothing would make me happier than to give you a clear field," he said. "Absolutely nothing. But I have a factory and a business with three hundred people and their families to think about. No, Sam, we can't risk it.

I can't have the plant all stirred up, with foremen rushing in here threatening to resign if you're not fired. The first thing you know, we'll have a good strike on our hands, and then we'll really be in the soup. We haven't had a strike since the big one in 1969, thank God, but that one just about ruined us. No, Sam, I think the best thing for you is to go back to your office and try to be the best personnel man in the state. And that means, son, that you will have to learn how to get along with foremen."

*   *   *

Sam's problem is an exceedingly perplexing one. On the one hand, he made a bold attempt to improve communication in the plant and actually succeeded as far as two departments were concerned. But he was not empathic enough. He did not sense what was going on in the other departments and he was not aware of the growing hostility the other foremen felt toward him.

Whether he can improve the situation by staying at Smith River is questionable. If he can enlist the help of the two foremen who have colllaborated with him, the three of them may be able, eventually, to break down the hostility that exists in the plant against more enlightened human relations, but it will be a long, slow painful job. It will be an uphill fight all the way against well-entrenched prejudice and tradition.

Another factor that cannot be dismissed lightly is the attitude of top management as represented by Mr. Bidwell. Mr. Bidwell wants employee turnover and absenteeism reduced, but not at the expense of the status quo. He would rather have things as they are than risk any major changes, even though these changes may be for the better. Since it is unlikely that Sam will change Mr. Bidwell's mind on this point, it might be wise for him to resign and to take his talents to an organization where they could be put to better use. It is very difficult to get people to communicate more effectively when they really do not want to.

CHAPTER TEN

Communication, Cohesiveness, and Morale

The Hillside Church is situated in a small town about twenty miles from a large city. Although it is only fifteen years old, it is already outgrowing its second building. If you watched the church go through a week's cycle, you would notice that there are activities going on all the time. Some of its meeting rooms are used three and four times a day. This is partly because the church serves as a kind of community center for many activities, like the Boy and Girl Scouts, the Mental Health Society, the Council of Cooperative Nursery Schools, and the League of Women Voters. But it is also because the members of the Hillside Church are very active people. Besides coming to church on Sunday to hear the minister, the average member of Hillside comes back to church once or twice a week to participate in committee meetings, group discusions, social concerns projects, potluck suppers, and a wide variety of activities which the church has organized and sponsored to meet the needs of its members. And as you watch the members come and go during the week, you are struck by the fact that they are, by and large, happy people. They have their problems and their disagreements but for the most part they appear to feel as though they are getting something out of life.

Now let us take a look at the boiler shop of the Metalcraft Iron Works. It is about 7:30 p.m., and the swing shift has stopped for lunch. As we go from group to group, the atmosphere is pleasant and relaxed. Bill the Blacksmith is giving a dramatic presentation of how he took top honors at bowling last night. He is really hamming it up and his audience is enjoying every minute of it. In another group, one of the riveters is complaining how the day shift keeps lousing everything up so that you spend the first three hours of your shift straightening things out before getting down to work. The other men in his group rather halfway agree with him but they are joking and making light remarks about what knuckleheads the day shift men are and are telling the riveter that he takes everything too seriously. We pass on to another group. A couple of layout men are engrossed in the problem of how to get an extra flange or two out of a sheet of boilerplate.

A half hour later, the gang is back at work. The atmosphere is still friendly and relaxed, even though the men are hard at work.

The congregation of the Hillside Church and the boilershop gang at the Metalcraft Iron Works are totally different groups, yet they have something in common. Somehow, the people who constitute these groups have found happiness and contentment in their association with each other. Working and meeting together is a friendly, creative experience for them. And the psychologist would say that the two groups rate high with regard to the factors of cohesiveness and morale.

When groups rate high in cohesiveness it means that they have a strong attraction or a "pull" for their members. They feel drawn together by a mutual attraction. In the two situations we have described, the members feel happy and comfortable within the group. They go to some trouble, make little sacrifices, and put up with inconveniences in order to participate with the group. Both the organizations we described have a low rate of absenteeism and turnover as compared to other, less cohesive groups.

Cohesiveness is sometimes called the "groupiness" factor—that force or condition that distinguishes a group from a collection of people. A movie audience does not have much cohesiveness because there is little feeling of mutual relationship among the individuals present. One of the reasons for this is that attending a movie affords few opportunities for interaction. In other words, the cohesiveness of a group will depend in part on the amount of communication between persons, upon the opportunities for self-expression and exchange of feeling.

Occasionally, we can watch the growth of cohesiveness in a large audience that is listening to a skilled lecturer. As the people come into the auditorium and sit down, they are largely strangers to each other. But as the lecturer begins to talk, he seems to draw the audience with him. His humorous remarks are greeted with laughter, and we note that each individual in the audience is not laughing separately by himself but *together* with the rest of the audience. The lecturer's quips and sallies unite the audience in the enjoyment of his humor. If the lecturer deals with an emotionally charged subject, he helps his listeners share fear, horror, amusement, pity, or whatever the theme of his topic may be. However, this kind of cohesiveness is a temporary phenomenon. Its effects largely disappear once the members of the audience have scattered to their homes.

Members of cohesive groups derive much of their satisfactions from sharing activities with other members. Shared activities are made possible by agreement on and conformity to specified patterns of behavior. Thus members of a chess club not only have a shared interest in playing chess, but they also adhere to the rules of the game, as well as to regulations—strict silence on the part of spectators, for example—that apply to the conduct of members. The cohesiveness of the group depends, in part, on their willingness to meet at certain times in a specified place, to pay dues, to elect officers, and spend most of their time together playing chess matches and discussing the lore of the game. Any members who would deviate markedly from rule and custom would constitute a source of distraction and would be encouraged to drop out of the club.

Every group that exists over an extended period of time develops behavioral norms—shared patterns of behavior—that characterize the actions of its members. Sometimes these norms are stated in formal terms—such as the time and place of meeting—but often they are tacit and informal, but nonetheless binding. The chess club, for example, may discourage the discussion of topics—politics, for instance—that might distract members from their main focus: chess. Membership in a really cohesive group is a satisfying and enriching experience, but it has a price: conformity to the group's norms.

*   *   *

When a group has one or more objectives that it considers to be worthwhile, and also feels that its activities contribute to those objectives, we say that it has high morale. High morale usually expresses itself in terms of optimism—a belief on the part of members that success will attend their efforts.

The members of the Hillside Church and the swing shift in the boiler shop of the Metalcraft Iron Works are optimistic about the outcome of the enterprises in which they are participating. They are optimistic about the continuance of the opportunity to come together with congenial people and to express themselves freely and creatively. These two objectives are in themselves very worth while, because they touch on two needs that are basic to human existence—the need for congenial social interaction and the need for creativity and self-expression. Above and beyond this, the goals get vague or, rather, they become difficult to express in words. Each of the groups has a feeling of "getting some place" or of "making progress," although if you asked the individuals making up the groups what "place" they were going to or what goal they were "making progress" toward, you would get a lot of different answers. In the church, some might talk of salvation or becoming a better person or of building a better world community. In the boiler-shop, some might talk about earning enough for a comfortable home or security or making things that are useful. In other groups characterized by high morale, the answers to these questions might be more easily expressed (although the basic reasons for high morale might be just as hard to put into words). This would be particularly true of a group participating in a hot political fight or of a team of scientists working on a piece of research or of a regiment at the front lines.

In the church group and the boiler-shop group we described, good group feeling is an end in itself and is accompanied, as we have said, by pleasantness and good fellowship. But there are many situations in life, perhaps even more common, where groups are cohesive and possess high morale for reasons that are negative rather than positive. One of the easiest ways to get people to work together is to frighten them. It is easier to organize people to combat a threat than it is to get them to work for something positive. The unity of a nation in time of war is an example of this. Perhaps this is one of the reasons why war has such a fatal attraction for the peoples of the world. In few other group activities do we get the sense of exhilaration or the opportunity to give ourselves completely to a cause. For a while it completely satisfies our need for participation in group enterprise.

On a smaller scale, we get much the same effect when citizens organize to eliminate corruption in local politics, or to prevent taxes from being raised, or to keep the price for rides on the merry-go-rounds in the city park from being raised to more than a nickel. The threat, the fear that an unwanted thing may happen, is enough to bring people together and to unify them in a joint cause, and as long as they feel they have a chance of winning—that is, as long as their morale is good—they will work and fight together.

Leaders have long been aware of the relationship between cohesion and morale on the one hand and the existence of a threatening situation on the other. Very often this relationship has been used by leaders to manipulate their followers. Dictators throughout history have justified their seizure of power on the grounds that forces of corruption and dissension within the government threatened the security of the nation. Thus General Idi Amin seized control of Uganda in 1971 (ousting Milton Obote, the prime minister who had assumed full power six years earlier) allegedly to protect the country from the internal dangers that threatened to overwhelm it. Amin singled out Asians (Indians and Pakistanis) as threats to the economy of Uganda, confiscated their assets, and expelled them. Amin was, however, only interested in unifying the tribespeople who supported him and he ruthlessly exterminated members of other tribes. His attempt to gain national support by attacking neighboring Tanzania backfired. Tanzanian troops counterattacked, invaded Uganda, and occupied the capital. Amin fled into exile. Dictators that attempt to build up cohesiveness and morale by scare tactics may succeed for brief periods, but they are usually destroyed by their excesses.

Generally speaking, as long as the goals of a group are negative—that is, as long as the purpose of the group is to defend itself against some thing or some one—its cohesiveness and morale are not very dependent on free communication and interaction. But if the goals of a group are positive, if they relate to such human needs as creativity, self-expression, and congenial social interaction, then cohesiveness and morale will depend on the ability of group members to communicate with each other and with their leaders. Blocks and bottlenecks in communication will worsen morale and break down cohesiveness. But if the situation becomes extremely difficult, members of the group may organize and challenge the established leadership which they have come to recognize as a threat to their security and well-being. The very act of their defiance will help them to develop cohesiveness.

For the most part, the activities we undertake with other people have positive rather than negative values for us. This is largely true of such things as shopping for food, attending PTA meetings, depositing money in the bank, voting, having the neighbors in for a friendly chat, and so forth. And it is particularly true of that activity that takes up such a large part of our lives—our everyday work. It is sometimes argued that the chief purpose of work is a negative one—to keep the wolf from the door, for example. And it may be that this analysis applies to people who heartily dislike their jobs and work at them only because they have to, and it may apply to people in impoverished situations, for whom like is a continuous struggle for existence. However, for most of us, working meets a great many more needs other than those associated with survival.

The point is, if we regard an employment situation—a factory, an office, a sales force, a hospital, or whatever—as one in which people work because they *have* to, because they have no choice, then we can say that it probably doesn't make much difference whether people are able to communicate or not, nor does the presence of morale or cohesiveness matter very much. But when people start looking to their work as a source of satisfaction and pride, when they become in any way emotionally involved in their work, and when they start to look upon the work situation as an opportunity to meet and to interact with congenial people, then they are going to be dissatisfied and frustrated if they cannot communicate easily with each other or with their bosses. And if they remain dissatisfied and frustrated in their work, morale and cohesion will suffer.

The particular contribution that the leader makes with respect to morale and cohesion in the group is what psychologists call "emotional climate." "Emotional climate" is a way of describing the kinds of feelings that group members are encouraged to have toward each other and particularly toward the leaders. These feelings in turn are largely influenced by the general behavior and attitudes of the leader. A leader who insists on making *all* decisions will generate a different kind of emotional climate than one who shares responsibility, encourages his subordinates to make decisions, and gives them freedom to do so. A leader whose communication with his subordinates takes the form of terse, abrupt memoranda will generate a different climate from the leader who communicates through the medium of the informal staff meeting.

The kind of climate that develops in an organization depends not only on the ways in which the leader communicates or acts but also on his values and attitudes. A genuinely democratic person can often convey this impression to his subordinates in spite of being required to use formalized methods of communication, and the true nature of an autocratic person is likely to show through his studied attempts to be democratic.

However, this does not mean that a person who has in the past made communication difficult in his organization cannot improve it. If he can understand that his tendencies to block communication are an expression of his personality, and if he can recognize the advantages of freer communication and will make a studied effort to remove the hazards that have made communication difficult, then he has a chance. The process will be difficult and long, and he will often meet with suspicion and misunderstanding on the part of those who worked under him before he decided to change his methods, but if he can stay with it long enough, he may be able to bring about some change in the kind of person he is and thus improve communication and morale. And this is one of the difficulties, one of the risks that discourage leaders from trying to make any real improvement in the kind of communication or the kind of emotional climate they generate: they sense that if the reform is carried out successfully, it will change their lives. They will not be the same people any more. This fear of change is one that has its roots in our earliest childhood and is one of the greatest handicaps to the improvement of communication in employment situations and in other human relationships.

*   *   *

It was 5:30 p.m. In a corner office on the third floor of a handsome granite building inscribed "Board of Education," George Graham, Ed.D., Superintendent of Schools for Greater Metropole, glanced moodily at a heavy folder his secretary had placed on his desk before she left for the day. It contained reports that he ought to go over before tonight's meeting of the Board of Education. Reading reports was about the last thing he felt like doing. What he really needed was a stiff drink, some of Mrs. Graham's excellent cooking, and a half hour's nap on the sofa. He looked at the folder again and groaned. The way things looked, he'd be lucky if he got home by midnight.

But he just wasn't in the mood for reports right now. The problems of the day were very much with him. The toughest one had been the high-school principals' meeting right after lunch. They were an unruly bunch to handle. Old Man Ryder was the ringleader. A couple of years ago the school system was surveyed by a committee from the University and one of the things that they had recommended was that Social Issues courses be put into all the high schools and required of all seniors. Some of the principals liked the idea and some of them didn't, but Old Man Ryder got his back up and said that Social Issues courses were a lot of progressive education hogwash, and if such a course were put into his school, it would be over his dead body. Dr. Graham secretly agreed with Ryder but the thing had already progressed too far. Besides, what Ryder was doing was insubordination. Well, the course was put into Ryder's school. It didn't go in over his dead body but it took a Board resolution specifically directing Mr. Ryder to set up a course in Social Issues and to see that all seniors take it. Naturally, Ryder didn't like that and he was out for the Superintendent's scalp.

Today he could tell they had something up their sleeves, but he had beat them to the punch. He told them about a plan one of the Board members had proposed to change the boundaries of the district served by each high school. Actually, Dr. Graham himself did not think much of the plan, but he presented it as though he felt it had some merit. He never did find out what the principals had cooked up to spring on him, because when he had finished telling them about the Board member's ideas on redistricting, the air was filled with anguished clamor. Each principal felt that the idea was directed at him, would not work, was unthinkable, and said so at length. Dr. Graham listened solemnly and said that he would pass their comments on to the Board member. By that time, the hour was almost up. He made a few routine announcements, thanked them all for coming, and walked out. He had escaped that one unscathed but it was a strain. He still wondered what kind of deal they were hatching. Well, as long as he could keep them off balance. . . .

His first appointment for the day had been with a group of parents representing the Mental Health Society of Greater Metropole, who had come to present a bill of complaints about the need for expanded and augmented psychological services for children. The Mental Health people were a kind of nuisance. He had tried to get them to talk to one of the assistant superintendents but they had insisted on seeing him in person. They were so intense and grim, they made him uncomfortable. Thank goodness, they didn't represent a very important element in town. He had been cool and polite and had pointed out that even if there were a need for a bigger staff of psychologists, it would be impossible to get an appropriation past the Board in their present mood. The Board was interested in finding a way to *save* money, not to spend more of it. When one of the visitors had said that he felt that the school system was unfriendly to the whole idea of mental health, Dr. Graham couldn't help pointing out that he was personally responsible for making Social Issues a required course in the high schools. He finally had to tell the committee that the interview was over.

His next interview was with some people from the teachers' association. Their complaint was that teachers were not getting enough time at lunch. Some of the schools had half-hour lunch periods, and when teachers were scheduled to supervise in the yard or in the halls, they had a bare ten or fifteen minutes in which to eat their lunch.

Dr. Graham tried to explain to the committee that this problem had come up several times before, but that it was out of his hands because it had been agreed that principals would be in charge of the scheduling of the time of their teachers. He urged them to take up the matter with the principals concerned, and when they answered that they had already done so without results, he could only repeat that the matter was out of his hands.

Dr. Corson, of Personnel and Research, had been in to see him next. Corson was a bright young fellow full of ideas but he had only been in Central Office for a couple of years and hadn't learned the ropes yet. Corson wanted to tell him about some idea for getting the teachers together for group discussions led by some of the supervisors and vice principals. Dr. Graham listened patiently for a while but then had to break in and tell Corson that it wouldn't work. Teachers just wouldn't stay on after four o'clock even if you had the Central Office staff doing handsprings to entertain them. Corson just didn't know these people the way he did. There was a lot Corson had to learn. He seemed downcast when he was told to forget the idea. Graham hated to say "no" all the time but if everybody would try to keep the ship afloat and on an even keel instead of dashing off in all directions, it would be a lot easier on the administration. Corson would turn out all right; he just needed seasoning.

One bright spot during the day was eating lunch with Charlie Howard. Charlie was in charge of buildings, grounds, and finance. He didn't have the headaches with Charlie that had with some of his other staff. Buildings and grounds stayed put. They weren't continually asking for priviliges and special consideration, they didn't get into trouble by slapping children, or by getting into fights with parents, or by joining the wrong political organizations. Charlie took care of his own problems; he wasn't always dropping them in the superintendent's lap. There had been some complaints about Charlie's department being inefficient but when you operated on a minimum budget, you had to expect some problems. The best thing about Charlie, though, was that he was good to talk to. Today he had talked to Charlie about the Grade School Teachers Association. They had been pestering him for more than a year about changing the curriculum in the elementary grades. They wanted to introduce more science. Every time they had come to see him, Dr. Graham had tried to talk them out of it, but they were getting more and more impatient. He was afraid that he couldn't hold them back much longer. One of these days they would be going over his head and appealing to the Board of Education, and when that happened. . . .

He shuddered to think. He and Charlie agreed that the last thing they needed right now was more science in the schools. There were plenty of important people in the community who thought that the schools were too heavily into science now, and some of them were on the Board of

Education. Charlie said that if the elementary school teachers would teach the curriculum they had now the way it ought to be taught, they wouldn't have time to go around stirring up trouble with talk of science education. Charlie was so right. But how do you get busybodies like the Grade School Teachers Association to mind their knitting?

Toward the end of the lunch hour he just happened on a way to solve the problem, and he and Charlie had a good laugh over it. The idea was that they would get old Holmes from the university to come over and do a survey of basic skills in the elementary grades. Holmes was always saying that nobody taught the fundamentals today the way they ought to be taught, so it was a foregone conclusion that he would find plenty of things wrong. If he could get the Board to go along with him on this, he would have the teachers just where he wanted them. They'd be so busy digging up ammunition to prove that they were right and Holmes was wrong, they'd forget all about this science ed silliness. Why, a fight about the fundamentals would be good for a couple of years at least. The newspapers would love it, and, if he played his cards right, he could take every trick.

As Dr. Graham sat in his office and looked out into the twilight, he began to feel a lot better. The day hadn't been such a bad one, after all. The prospect of having Professor Holmes do a survey had even more merit than he had thought at first. Why, he could even get Holmes to survey the whole school system, and then he'd have the whole bunch—teachers and principals—on the run. Tomorrow he'd have a press conference and say that he was concerned, *greatly* concerned, about the quality of teaching in the Greater Metropole schools. He'd talk with Corson the first thing in the morning and see what statistics he could get together to build up the idea. Then, after the newspapers had kicked it around for a week, he'd suggest that the Board hire Holmes to do the survey. Holmes would be delighted of course; he'd been complaining for years that no one would listen to him.

He slipped the reports in his briefcase, slipped on his overcoat, and headed for the door. If he left now, he could go home for dinner and be back for the Board meeting at eight. It might be a good idea to drop a few hints tonight touching on his concern about the quality of teaching in the schools. What would be a good businesslike way to catch their interest? Ah, he had it. "It's about time we took stock. . . ."

* * *

Dr. Graham is a phenomenon of the twentieth century—a school administrator, a leader who is caught between the pressures of an articulate public, an articulate profession, and an articulate board of education. Everyone seems to consider himself an expert in the field of education, and superintendents of schools and boards of education probably get more different kinds of contradictory advice over any given period of time than any other group of administrative officials in the country. Hence a great deal of the difficulty Dr. Graham encounters in trying to be an effective leader stems from the confusion that naturally results when one is the focus for so many conflicting pressures. Dr. Graham, of course, sees his job as one of coping with these pressures, allying himself with the forces that are the most powerful, and playing off the weaker forces against each other. He would probably say that he does this in order to keep the educational machinery functioning. However, he tends to lose sight of some of the more basic functions of his office—to meet the educational needs of children, to translate the basic educational policies of the community into practice, and to provide professional leadership for the teachers under his direction and control. Instead he concentrates most of his attention on manipulating the situation and the people around him in order to keep the power under his control.

One of the strongest criticisms that we can make of Dr. Graham from the standpoint of effective leadership is that he goes to great lengths to prevent communication from taking place. To be sure, he does want information from principals and teachers, but only certain, specified information. He does not want teachers to tell him that they do not have enough time for lunch, because he feels they should buckle down and do their jobs and not waste time complaining. Nor is he interested in parents telling him that psychological services need expanding. He wants to be the one to decide what services need expanding and he resents being told what they should be.

Dr. Corson's suggestion regarding discussion groups composed of teachers and administrators has merit from the standpoint of effective leadership, because it would provide opportunities for better communication. Perhaps this is one of the reasons why Dr. Graham is against it; he is afraid of what might happen if teachers start to communicate freely with each other and with administrators. Furthermore, he is afraid of any situation that he does not control absolutely, and who knows what disturbing ideas might come from such meetings?

The Grade School Teachers Association wants to redesign the elementary school curriculum by bringing in more material of a scientific nature. This suggestion has threatening possibilities for Dr. Graham. "Science education" is controversial in Greater Metropole, because of the implication that evolutionary theories of biology might be taught, and if the teachers went ahead with their plan, it would put Dr. Graham on the defensive. Perhaps most of the community does not care how much science there is in the curriculum. Perhaps there are a few who would favor more science and a few who would not, but the few who would oppose it would make life very difficult, and Dr. Graham feels that he has enough to do to keep the school system operating, let alone defending something he personally doesn't support, anyhow.

Another reason he is against their proposal is that he does not favor teachers deciding what changes should be made in the curriculum. That is something for the Central Office of the schools to decide, and Dr. Graham regards it as presumptuous for the teachers to think that they should take the lead in this.

Because Dr. Graham is not interested in improving communication in the school department, but rather in preventing and blocking it, and because he is more concerned about maintaining his power and authority than in carrying out the more basic functions of his office, the morale in the Greater Metropole schools is poor. Teachers see their jobs as chores rather than challenges. They lack cohesion in professional matters; they have lost the hope and the interest that brought them into teaching originally. The Grade School Teachers Association is one of the last groups that is interested in promoting professional growth, and if they fail in their move to revise the elementary curriculum, they will lose what little power and status they have. The teachers are beginning to develop cohesiveness only when they feel that they are under attack or when they feel that they are being deprived of a right or privilege that is important to them. The threat of a lay off will unite them, or they may try to use their united numbers to get a more liberal lunch hour out of the Board of Education.

Many of them envy the teachers in nearby smaller communities whose morale is much higher and who work in school systems that are more democratically organized. But the pay is higher in Greater Metropole, so they stay on.

Leaders like Dr. Graham are not confined to school systems, of course. We find them everywhere—in business and industry, in hospitals, labor unions, churches, government agencies, fraternal organizations— wherever people come together and form organizations. The leaders we put in charge of these organizations have to have power to carry out their administrative functions, to provide the services we demand, and to attain the objectives we had in mind when we created the organizations. Inadequate administrators are likely to focus on caretaking aspects of their job and to ignore the goals for which their organizations were constituted. And when they come under criticism, they are likely to complain that they do not have enough power to accomplish what is expected of them.

This seems to be Dr. Graham's problem. He is confused because he is a small man in a big job, a man who does not possess the breadth of thought and insight that is needed to understand his *whole* job. Hence he becomes preoccupied with one aspect of his situation—the power factor.

Still another possibility is that he is a person who has rather severe emotional problems. If so, these problems would not necessarily appear on the surface; very likely he would give the *appearance* of a friendly, pleasant individual, somewhat harried and overworked, but having no special difficulties. And *he* would not be aware that he had any emotional problems. Instead, he would just be aware of the continual need to struggle for power, to keep his subordinates in their place, to deny human values. Indeed, most professional workers who deal with problems of mental health are convinced that the condition of being preoccupied with power is actually a form of neurosis.

The leader who prevents, instead of facilitates, free communication does so principally because of emotional reasons rather than because of lack of sufficient knowledge or information. To permit free communication leads inevitably to the sharing of power and authority. The insecure, anxious, and inadequate leader *never* feels that he has enough power; hence any suggestion that he share it with his subordinates is viewed by him as a threat to his personal security. Permitting free communication also implies that people will be freer to express hostility openly, and the insecure leader finds it difficult or impossible to tolerate the anxiety he will feel when and if this occurs. Where hostility is concerned, his motto: "Out of sight, out of mind."

Because the resistance of many leaders to the idea of free communication has its roots deep in the emotional side of life, any attempts to bring about changes for the better must take this fact into consideration. This is why it is not possible to make people into better leaders, or change them from communication-blockers to communication-facilitators, simply by giving them a one-week course in human relations or by having them sit through a series of lectures on how to improve morale.

About all these approaches can do is to *prepare* people for more effective leadership by indicating some of the problems and by pointing out some of the ways that the problems might be handled. The *actual change* in the behavior of a leader will come after he has become completely convinced of the correctness of the new approach and has worked it into his way of dealing with his subordinates over a period of months or more likely, years.[1] In this, he needs the continual support of like-minded people. It is too much to expect that an individual change his pattern of leadership *all by himself.* He needs the help of sympathetic and understanding people, preferably other leaders, to talk through the problems he meets with in attempting to reorganize his thinking and his behavior. Otherwise, he has no check on himself, otherwise the frustrations and disappointments that are inevitable when one undertakes personal reform prove too difficult to handle, and one tends to drift back into less-adequate modes of behavior.

In some organizations, reforms have been carried through successfully with the help of teams of psychological consultants. Some teams begin with interviews with the top managerial personnel, in order to determine what their goals, perspectives, and difficulties are. As team members interview people at successively lower levels, they arrange for meetings that serve the purpose of enabling individuals at various levels of management to clarify aims and to resolve problems of communication. Other organizations have staff psychologists who engage in similar activities—a process known as organizational development. Seminars held away from work for brief perods of time are also used in organizational development. Still other managerial staff members conduct their education in human relations less systematically—with a mixture of reading, seminar and conference attendance, and enrollment in special courses, as well as by meeting informally from time to time with other administrators and executives with whom they share a common interest in improving the working environment of their organizations or groups. It is important to note that the persons in authority who have been successful in improving communication, morale, and group feeling among their subordinates are the ones who continue the process of education over a period of years (in many cases, throughout their professional careers) and who also do not attempt the job alone, but instead discuss issues and problems with both professionally trained psychologists and other administrators and executives.

FOOTNOTE CHAPTER 10

[1]See S.L. Tubbs and R.N. Widgery, When productivity lags, check at the top: Are key managers really communicating? *Management Review*, Nov. 1978, pp. 20-25

CHAPTER ELEVEN

Signposts on the Road to Effective Leadership

It is difficult or impossible to be an effective leader without continuing to grow psychologically. This means that the effective leader must set the task for himself of increasing his understanding both of himself and those around him. It also means that he must continually look for better ways of dealing with the problems that are bound to occur when people work and play together. The leader who is no longer interested in finding better ways of handling situations and who does not discover ever-deepening insights into why people behave as they do is a leader who is in danger of deteriorating, or becoming less effective.

What we shall attempt to do in this chapter is to indicate and discuss a number of directions or ways in which leaders need to grow if they are to become effective or if they are to continue to be effective. Most of us are capable of making lists of things we ought to be doing, and if this discussion becomes merely another list of "ought's" and "should's," then it has failed its purpose. But if, on the other hand, it helps the reader to examine himself critically and if it arouses enough "normal anxiety" to promote a re-evaluation of relations with others, it will have served its purpose.

*   *   *

Picking up the theme of the last chapter, it is evident that leaders need to learn how to communicate more effectively and to make communication possible, because good communication is vital to cohesion, morale, and the kind of emotional climate that generates satisfying and effective group relationships.

In our recent discussion of communication, we omitted mention of one of the leader's important functions, that of communicating to persons outside the immediate group for which he is responsible. This includes his superiors and anyone else who is interested or who ought to be interested in the activities of the group. Much the same principles apply here as apply to communication within the group or organization. In order to communicate to others, one must be a good listener, must be empathic, and so on. However, the relationship is not usually as close as it is with members of the organization nor are others expected to be as deeply involved in an emotional sense. Sometimes this means that communication must be on a more superficial plane, sometimes it means that special care must be taken to express oneself economically and interestingly. One of the most effective ways to get the attention of audiences is, of course, to show them how what you have to say affects them personally. People are likely to give better attention to matters in which they are personally involved.

The reason we make special mention of this dimension of communication is that some leaders give a great deal of attention to developing communication with persons outside the group who may have a vital effect on the group's welfare. Few groups, if any, are completely isolated. Even if there are no individuals outside the group who have a direct effect on the welfare of the group, there are ways in which the attitudes and opinions of others can produce subtle changes. For example, how the members of a group or organization feel about themselves as members is closely related to how outsiders feel about the group. In other words, the morale and cohesion of a group usually bears a relationship to the public's attitudes.

The U.S. Navy applied this principle in building up the prestige of the Submarine Service during World War II. The fact that both naval personnel and the public at large came to look upon the Submarine Service with respect, appreciation, and admiration was a large factor in developing and maintaining the morale and feeling of group pride that characterized submariners, generally, during the Second World War. Submarine duty is a close, confining, monotonous kind of life, and the strong, positive group feeling that was developed among persons assigned to this duty went a long way in helping to compensate for these difficulties. The fact that the Navy gave submariners extra pay was, to be sure, a material reward, but the status that one receives from being *entitled* to draw extra pay is of greater psychological value than the material advantages resulting from having more money.

The morale and cohesiveness exhibited by submariners was quite in contrast during World War II to the low morale and lack of group feeling among personnel assigned to amphibious duty—to landing craft. During the initial years of the war, the Navy overlooked the desirability of giving special attention to morale in this arm of the service. The Navy realized its error later, when it discovered that amphibious personnel felt themselves to have the lowest status of any arm of the naval service. They felt that they had been "forgotten" by the rest of the Navy, that amphibious duty was a catch-all for misfits, and that the other branches of the naval service were better equipped, better manned, and received better all-around care. Inasmuch as the amphibious forces provided a crucial and vital service, due to the kind of warfare that was waged in World War II, the discovery of low morale among amphibious personnel became a matter of great concern. As a result of this disclosure, the Navy attempted to build up the morale of this "forgotten" group by such devices as permitting the wearing of an identifying shoulder patch and by giving special attention to the needs and demands of this branch of the naval service. Undoubtedly these measures helped, although amphibious personnel never developed the spirit that was characteristic of other branches of the Navy—the Submarine Service, Naval Aviation, and the Marine Corps.

When the morale of personnel assigned to amphibious craft deteriorated, they were only reflecting the low opinion of their branch held by other naval personnel, and when the morale of other branches was high, it, too, was a reflection of the opinion of the rest of the Navy, as well as of the general public.

Morale and cohesion are often developed as a by-product of competition, but this does not mean that competition is essential or that morale and cohesion are developed by some units of a group or organization necessarily at the expense of other units. If the leadership of a group is operating effectively, and if the general climate in which both leader and group must function is favorable, it is possible for *all* units or subgroups to cevelop high morale and good group feeling. And when we say that the leader is operating effectively, we mean in part that he is able to communicate effectively and to make communication possible within his group or organization, as well as with others outside his group or organization.

*   *   *

As authority figures develop more effective leadership skills, they generally broaden their understanding of what we might variously describe as the power relationships, the internal dynamics and processes, or the operating functions of his group as well as of the other groups that bear some kind of relationship to his.

In a group of workers, this means that the supervisor will know which workers have the greatest influence with the other workers. He knows how he stands with his workers—what things they want him to do without bothering them and what things they want to talk over first. He knows, too, how he stands with his bosses—where he can go to get action, where he can go for support, and to whom he can go if he just wants to talk things over. He knows what the channels are for getting things done.

It is important that the leader see and understand these things because a leader who ignores the psychological facts of his situation is asking for frustration and failure. Let us look at a couple of examples.

When Hal Darcy asked Frank Simpson to act as a straw boss in assembling and installing the new unit, he didn't know he was asking for trouble. He picked Frank because he had been in the shop a long time and because he had more education than the other fellows. What he didn't know was that Frank was resented and disliked. Or, rather, he knew in a vague way that Frank was often at odds with the other fellows, but he never thought it was very important. Well, the new unit was installed, but it took twice as long as it should have. Shortly thereafter, two of the men quit. For a couple of weeks, production in the shop was down and spoilage was up.

*   *   *

Lt. Bonesteel signed his name at the bottom of a typed document, put it in an envelope, and handed it to the waiting orderly.

"Be sure that this gets to the colonel before lunch," he directed.

As the orderly left, Bonesteel turned toward his visitor, Lt. Irene Ivers.

"Well, I've done my good turn for today," he said with a laugh, "but if it's like my other good turns, nothing will come of it."

The other officer looked puzzled.

"What do you mean?" she asked.

"I asked to have Kowalski okayed for training in electronics," he replied. "He's a good kid—a hard worker and sharp as a whip. But the colonel has bounced every request like this I've sent him. Says we're undermanned at this post and the people we get for replacements get worse every month."

"The colonel could be right," laughed Ivers. "He's been right before." Then, more seriously, she asked, "Tell me, is that how you send requests like this through? Just send them over by orderly?"

"Why not?" Bonesteel asked. "Oh, I suppose I could take the matter up with the colonel personally but you know how he is about these things. He just sits and lets you talk and then thanks you for coming in and that's all. You don't know where you stand or anything. I'd feel like a fool going in to see him, unless it was something awfully important."

"I think I understand how you feel," said Ivers. "But I didn't mean that you should take this up personally with the colonel. What I meant was, just sending him a letter like this isn't the way you do it. I sent two of my people to foreign language school last month, and another is going to be sent away for special training in computer programming tomorrow."

Bonesteel raised his eyebrows.

"You don't say!" he exclaimed. "What's the secret of your success?"

Ivers smiled. "There's no secret. I guess you're just the only one on the post that doesn't know how to get something through the colonel. Just see Margaret Winslow."

Bonesteel looked amazed. "You mean the sergeant in the colonel's office?"

Ivers was enjoying herself. "Sure. The same. The very same one." She chuckled. Bonesteel was *so* uptight, *so* proper. Of course, he wouldn't have thought of taking his problems to a sergeant. Particularly a woman sergeant like Winslow. She watched Bonesteel's puzzled expression turn into a frown.

"Oh, don't go hauling out the regulations," Ivers said, good humoredly. "It's very simple. Winslow is capable and the colonel knows it. She goes over the morning mail and sorts it out. The things she knows are important she puts on top with an orange sticker. The rest go underneath. When the colonel is rushed, as he is these days, she writes notes, boiling the substance of each letter down to a sentence. Sometimes she even adds: 'Good idea' or 'Lousy idea.' But she only does this when she has gone into the matter pretty thoroughly because the colonel trusts her judgment. Of course, I don't know what happens to your letters, but from what has happened in the past, I think you ought to see Winslow."

Bonesteel continued to frown.

"I don't think it's right," he said. "It's 'way out of authorized channels."

"How very true," said Ivers, sardonically, "but you know as well as I do that if we used authorized channels all the time, the work'd never get done."

*   *   *

Lt. Ivers is exaggerating, of course, largely for effect, because a great deal of the work of the Army and other organizations is carried out by people using authorized channels. But what Ivers means is that there is another set of channels that are officially recognized, but nevertheless used by personnel in the organization when official channels do not work. This *un*official recognition gives them a kind of legitimacy in the eyes of those who use them.

Hal Darcy and Lt. Bonesteel are making the error of confusing the situation as it *ought* to be with the situation as it exists. Hal does the obvious thing of picking Frank Simpson because of his experience and education, and Lt. Bonesteel does the obvious thing of sending his letter through channels, without clearing through Sgt. Winslow. Their "map" of the situation does not correspond with reality, and they are confused and frustrated when things do not turn out as they should.

Leaders owe it to themselves and their groups or organizations to be aware of such realities. We are not suggesting that leaders should counsel their followers to engage in behavior that is illegal or unethical or immoral, but what we are saying is that leaders should be well aware of the informal as well as the formal ways of getting things done, because the former is often more important than the latter. We are saying, too, that leaders should be keenly aware that what people say "officially"—for publication and circulation—is very often what they want others to believe or what they would really like to believe themselves. A leader who takes people too literally is not likely to be a very effective leader. This does not mean that leaders should be cynical or should lose faith in people, because we believe, on the contrary, that effective leaders are individuals who develop greater and deeper faith in people, the longer they work at being leaders. What we do mean is that what people say and what they do may each be related to different needs or purposes.

A man may come to a foreman and say that he is quitting for reasons of poor health. His real reason may be: "I can't get along with my fellow workers," or "I can't seem to get along with you as a supervisor." He uses the excuse of poor health as a blind because he does not want to discuss a problem that is painful or embarrassing. If the foreman is perceptive and realizes what is behind the request, he may decide to accept the excuse at face value out of consideration for the feelings of the individual, or he may decide to take some action that may make it unnecessary for the worker to quit.

When we prescribe official channels for communicating and getting things done, we are satisfying our need to make things logical, to make them fit our idea of the established order of things. This is a very real need, for we get a certain sense of security out of having things orderly and presumably predictable. But the trouble is, the system cannot accommodate all the problems that the organization develops. Or it does not permit adequate communication. Or one or two people, because of their personality, constitute bottlenecks. If the morale of the organization is good, if its people really want to get the job done, they will develop unofficial ways of solving their problems. So they satisfy their need for security by developing a system of official channels which they use part of the time, and they satisfy their need to get things done by using unofficial channels when official channels do not meet their needs.

All of this puts the leader in an ambiguous position, of course. On the one hand, he may be the official representative of the administration, but on the other hand, his chief role is to help the group work toward its goals and objectives—to get things done. Sometimes these roles are incompatible, and the leader must decide which comes first. However he resolves such problems, he must keep a firm grip on reality as well as on the values that govern the behavior of his group or organization.

*   *   *

We have made a great deal in this book of the hostility that is directed toward leaders, particularly in this country. Some leaders have learned how to handle the problem of hostility; others have not. Becoming a target for hostility can be a shattering experience. People who undertake leadership roles for the first time (and sometimes even persons who are experienced leaders) are often shocked or upset when they discover hostility and resistance among their subordinates. They wonder whether it is directed at them personally, whether they are ineffectual leaders, whether they have failed, or whether they are misinterpreting what goes on in their groups. And then there is the hostility that is submerged or passive and does not appear on the surface but operates as apathy or boredom or over-conformity or in some similarly frustrating form. Most of us, as we have said before, are made anxious by the hostility of others. Hence it is difficult to be an effective leader when one is the target of hostility.

It is hard to say which is worse—to be overly sensitive to hostility or to be unaware of its existence. Either condition leads to difficulties, and the effective leader is one who learns to expect and to accept the hostility that is directed toward him and who at the same time learns to be less vulnerable, less easily disturbed by it. Becoming less vulnerable, of course, is not something one practices as a separate skill. Rather, it is an inseparable part of the larger task of becoming an effective leader. As we come to feel more adequate and more capable, as we have repeated successes in playing our leadership roles, we find ourselves less annoyed at discovering evidence of hostility. We learn to accept hostility as an inevitable part of being a leader, and, if we are leaders in certain kinds of groups, we will prefer to begin with a group that is slightly hostile because it means that the group is capable of developing a drive and spirit that is not found in more passive groups.

Accepting the more or less openly expressed hostility of a group is often a useful way of furthering one's acceptance as a leader and helping to promote better feeling in the group. An example from the experience of a psychology instructor I know may help to illustrate.

A common belief that one encounters among students (and other lay people, for that matter) is that psychologists universally recommend that children never be spanked. Sometimes this gets to be a kind of symbolic barrier for students, who use is as a justification for rejecting anything that a psychologist might say. Such an individual says to himself in effect: "Since psychologists are so silly and unrealistic as to say that children should never be spanked, I cannot go along with anything else they might say." More than once the issue of whether children should be spanked has been raised by representatives of little subgroups in my friend's psychology classes. These are usually the people who not only reject psychology and psychologists but are resentful of the fact that they must take a required course in psychology. The question usually comes up when the instructor has made the point in one of his lectures that he thinks parents punish primarily to relieve their own feelings and that it they are really honest with themselves they would have to admit that the welfare of the child is for the moment a secondary consideration. At this point one of this small group of rebels is likely to ask with a taunting note in his voice:

"Do you spank your children?"

This is an overtly hostile challenge. The purpose of this question is to put the professor in an embarrassing position. If he says "No," he is just like all psychologists—a little softheaded. If he says "Yes," he obviously does not practice what students believe (erroneously) he has been preaching. His routine reply to this question is:

"Only in anger."

This always gets a laugh from the class, a friendly laugh, not a laugh of derision, a laugh that relieves the tension that has been aroused by the attack on the instructor. The answer shows the class that he recognizes the hostile character of the remark and that he can accept and withstand the expression of hostility without being unduly upset. The remark also shows that he is human and fallible and can admit his fallibility. This, too, helps the group to relax because they no longer feel that he is trying to get them to conform to impossible standards of behavior.

The same instructor had a student in an advanced class, a very bright young man and the member of a minority group that is struggling to make progress against all the handicaps that prejudice can place in its path. This young man, whom we shall call Mr. Smith, carried the proverbial chip on his shoulder. Inasmuch as the instructor was a person in authority, a person who seemed to represent people who dominate our national life and are hence responsible for the prejudice expressed toward minority groups, he inevitably came in for his share of Mr. Smith's hostility. The method used by the student was to make critical remarks in a low voice whenever he felt that the instructor was taking advantage of his position or making unjust or undue demands on the class. The instructor tried to ignore this behavior at first. He recognized the reasons why the student behaved as he did, and besides, there was nothing that the student said that was directly disrespectful. Yet the frequent criticism got under his skin.

One day, the instructor came to class five minutes late on a day he had scheduled an examination. As he handed out the examinations, Mr. Smith murmured accusingly:

"I suppose you know this gives us only 45 minutes to complete this test."

The instructor gritted his teeth. The remark in itself was inoffensive, but coming after some seven weeks of "needling," he felt that it was time to say something. So he smiled and, looking directly at the student, he replied:

"Mr. Smith, did you ever hurt yourself with your own needle?"

Mr. Smith looked surprised and momentarily confused and said, yes, sometimes he did.

Ten minutes later, the instructor noticed that the sun had gone behind the clouds and that the classroom was getting dark, so he went over to the door and switched on the lights. The class took no notice of this but went on writing their examinations. Only Mr. Smith glanced up from his paper and, looking at the instructor, said appreciatively:

"Thank you."

One of the points demonstrated by this anecdote is that subordinates and group members very likely are unaware that their behavior is as hostile as it is. When the instructor replied to Mr. Smith, he was saying in effect: "I'm making a sort of joke of your remark, but I recognize its inherent hostility.

But I will not take advantage of my position to punish or humiliate you."

Mr. Smith got the point, and it brought him up sharply because he had been unaware of the hostile nature of his behavior. Basically, he was a sensible person and he knew that he had no realistic reason to fear the instructor or to punish him for the prejudice society had displayed toward his people. And his recognition of the instructor's thoughtful gesture was apparently a way of admitting his error and recognizing the instructor as a person of good will.

It is much more important for leaders to handle hostility of group members or subordinates skillfully in these times than it was in bygone eras. Formerly, leaders were expected to deal drastically and forcefully with any evidence of hostility. Harshness and severity were considered to be characteristic of leaders. Machiavelli admonished his prince, for example, that it is better to be feared than to be loved.

Today, however, we are much less inclined to tolerate harsh and drastic behavior on the part of our leaders. The rights of leaders and the rights of the consumers of leadership are each on a far more equal basis, and the leader who chronically retaliates and who punishes the expression of hostility too severely is likely to find himself deposed or removed from his office or to have all kinds of trouble getting his people to do what is expected and required of them.

In other words, the leader of today, whether he likes it or not, must live with a great deal more openly expressed hostility than the leaders of former days. This is true of people in leadership positions everywhere, regardless of whether they are business executives, doctors, foremen, teachers, policemen, social workers, or whatever. It is very likely that the ability to withstand and to cope with hostility has become a kind of test of leadership. Perhaps we, as members of a group, have the feeling that if a leader can not only stand up to our expressions of hostility but can help us turn our hostile drives into constructive action, he has merited our support and cooperation.

*   *   *

People who are effective leaders invariably have some kind of emotional appeal for those they guide or supervise. The kind of appeal differs with each leader's personality as well as with the kind of position he holds. It is probably more important for a priest or a teacher to inspire others than it is for a lawyer, dentist, or a social worker, yet the difference is one of degree rather than of its absence or presence. The teacher or the priest who is effective inspires his audience to want to be like him in some ways, whereas the lawyer or the social worker inspires his client to want to follow his advice or to take certain actions. And, in any event, the effective leader inspires his audience to give him their attention and to listen.

A basic principle that underlies any emotional attraction a leader has for his following is that he must be able to be or say or do something that others perceive to be of value to them or to apply to them. We go to dentists, take courses from teachers, or contact government officials because we are looking for help with some of our problems. We ask certain group members to become presidents or chairmen because we need someone to moderate the group, help it operate, represent it, and take responsibility for its functioning. If these people carry through their assignments in an offhand manner and without obvious commitment, we are dissatisfied. But if they are able to give us the feeling that they are interested in our welfare, that our problems are important to them, then we are more likely to accept them and to give them our loyalty. They have made an emotional investment in us, and we in turn are willing to do what they want us to do, to try to change in the direction that they want us to change. We have such feelings as "I wish I could be like him," or "He is really one of us."

Developing this kind of feeling among others is not only an art, it is a way of life. Some leaders develop it only superficially, because they are interested in accumulating power for themselves and are unwilling or unable to give others the help and the attention they need and want. This is often what happens when individuals feel that all that is necessary to be an effective leader is to possess charisma—to be charming and popular, or dynamic and overwhelming. As we have indicated previously, some of the hostility that leaders face is the result of previous disappointments experienced by group members at the hands of leaders who were only interested in exploiting their subordinates or who were just not equal to the demands and responsibilities of the leadership role.

A really effective leader is able to command attention and to inspire his following because he has a secure feeling of what he is and what he can do, and this usually means that he has a good idea of what he is not and what he cannot do. He conveys these ideas to subordinates by what he says and does, and particularly by his attitude of respect and appreciation for the value and worth of other people. He shows this respect and appreciation by being willing to listen to people, by taking infinite pains to see that communication is made possible, by not using his power and authority to crush or humiliate the person who expresses his hostility openly. Conversely, he expects others to accept and respect him as an individual and not merely because of his status as a leader.

An effective leader inspires and reassures us because he symbolizes the best that is in us. He may fall far short of our ideals just as *we* fall short of them, but we admire his ability to progress in the desired direction and to encourage us to do likewise.

Leaders who inspire us in this way are encouraging what Albert Bandura[1] of Stanford University calls "social learning"—our inclination to imitate the behavior of those individuals who are psychologically significant to us. Social learning continues throughout the life span, and it is through imitating the behavior of persons who are important to us—

parents, admired relatives, friends, teachers, religious leaders, and even bosses and political figures—that we become socially competent. In addition to the skills that make up this competency, we also learn the values and attitudes that encourage the development and practice of these skills. Thus individuals in positions of leadership, authority, and prestige serve as models for those who are their followers, subordinates, or admirers.

One of the most effective ways a leader can reassure and inspire is by sharing his power, by permitting and encouraging subordinates or group members to participate with him in making decisions and in carrying out important functions.

The leader who can share power successfully thereby tells his following in effect that he has confidence in them. Because of his trust in them, they are encouraged to become more adequate and more competent.

The sharing of power is an answer to the open expression of hostility. It is a way of meeting the challenge openly, of meeting the objectors more than halfway. To the person who demands in effect, "By what right do you make decisions for us and tell us what to do?" the leader replies, "How would you like to share in the making of decisions?"

What happens all too often, when decision-making and policy-making are monopolized by leaders, is that the rest of the group or organization feels absolved of responsibility. If something goes wrong or if the goals are not attained, it is the leader's fault. *He* is responsible; let *him* worry about the mess. This is, of course, contrary to principles of good group management. In a group or organization that is productive, that is making progress toward its goals, an individual member must take some responsibility for doing his part, for investing some of himself in the group. Thus, the employee who sees himself as merely "a cog in the machine" will feel no sense of urgency or responsibility when he sees a generator start to burn out its bearings. He is supposed to attend to *his* machine; the generator is someone else's responsibility—another worker's or the foreman's. Let someone else worry about it. Perhaps he takes a little malicious pleasure in seeing this happen; his lack of outward concern is his revenge for not being considered important enough to share in decision making and planning.

On the other hand, when subordinates and group members *do* participate in the making of policy and decisions, they are much more likely to take some responsibility upon themselves for carrying out both policy and decisions. Furthermore, they feel a greater sense of identity with the organization, so that when they see a way to economize, boost sales, or report some valuable information to the group, they take some initiative in doing so.

Specifically, what does power-sharing mean when translated into the everyday relations between leaders and the consumers of leadership?

It means that the professional worker does not hide behind a barrage of technical language in making explanations to patients or clients. It means that he takes some responsibility to see that they understand the nature of their problems at least to the extent that they are in a position to make some decisions about them.

It means that the teacher gives students opportunities to think through problems raised by the course material, to ask or raise questions, and to communicate with him.

It means that the executive both encourages and permits employees to participate directly or through representation in the making of decisions that affect their lives or their work.

Now, all this does not mean that the leader abdicates *all* or even most of his power, authority, and responsibility. For one thing, leaders generally are responsible to other agencies and to people above and beyond the groups they supervise or aid. The doctor, for example, has a responsibility to the medical profession, to society, and to himself. The business executive has a responsibility to the board of directors, the public who consumes the product or uses the services his company provides, and, of course, to himself. The degrees and kinds of responsibility vary with different kinds of leaders. The tax assessor's responsibility to his superiors and to the government agency that employs him is much stronger than his responsibility to the individual whose property he is appraising. The discussion leader's responsibility is primarily to his group. Consequently, the assessor will share very little of his power, whereas the effective group leader will share as much as he can—as much as is consistent with the best interests of his group and the people who compose it.

This brings up the problem of how much power can be reasonably shared. A great many people have grown up to believe that the best of all arrangements is for the leader to have all the power and to take all the responsibility, and they are shocked and upset by being given responsibility and freedom to think and act. When such people constitute a small minority of a group that is willing to participate in power-sharing, this does not make much of a problem because they are usually carried along with the rest of the group and often attain real growth and maturity as a result of this experience. However, when people of this type dominate the group, or when they are able to raise the anxieties of the other members of the group to such a point that they seriously affect cohesiveness and morale, then they will constitute a real threat to the productivity of the group. This is a severe test of the effectiveness of the leader. If he can meet this challenge with firmness and friendliness and see that all channels of communication are open and operating, he can turn an uncomfortable, disagreeable situation into a victory for himself and for the group.

There is, of course, the danger of progressing too fast, as Sam Raton did in the Smith River Furniture Company. The kinds of people we described in that anecdote are not ready for direct and immediate power-sharing. They have to be educated to the point where they are ready to take their share of decision-making and responsibility. Such a process of education makes great demands on the leader in terms of time, patience, sensitivity, and empathy. He must be able to sense how far he can push reforms without arousing too much anxiety and without jeopardizing the morale and cohesiveness that the group or organization already possesses. On the other hand, he should be able to arouse enough *normal* anxiety to make the group want to progress. Some groups will make more progress than others. A supervisor of a group of workers in, say, Arabia, where autocratic, authoritarian ways of life are an integral part of the culture, will need to be very cautious about instituting reform. However, this does not mean that he abandon all idea of helping his Arab subordinates to take responsibility and to share in decision-making. There are ways of subtly involving people in these processes, virtually without their knowing that they are involved. Furthermore, most cultures have customs that fit in well with the development of enlightened human relations. For example, the idea that a ruler or leader should be available to petition by the humblest person, a custom that is well fixed and respected in the Arab cultures, is one that may be used to good advantage in improving communication.

In the final analysis, people normally and naturally want to be cooperating members of a group, participating in its decisions as well as in its everyday functions and operations. The difficulty is that so many have been taught to behave and believe differently by childhood experiences or by the culture in which they live. The leader who lives in a society or culture which has a friendly attitude toward democratic principles, where the freedom and the essential worth of each individual are important, will have less difficulty in setting up a system for sharing power and responsibility. Indeed, there will be pressures on him to make some provision for power-sharing if he is reluctant to do so.

Many leaders are reluctant to share power because they are fearful of developing potential leaders who may compete with them. However, a leader who is really honest with himself will take that risk because he will be able to say that the group or organization deserves the best leadership it can get. In actuality, it seldom happens that a leader who demonstrates his effectiveness by sharing power is eliminated or by-passed. What does happen is that the affairs of the group or organization make better progress, because group members take more personal responsibility for the success of their joint undertaking.

The effective leader shares his power not only because he has found this method to be a more efficient way of getting things done but also because by recognizing the leadership talent that is latent in his subordinates, he builds up their sense of adequacy and personal competence. Hence they are less likely to feel resentful and exploited. By sharing his power, he shows that he is not afraid to share it and that he is not anxious and insecure, for only a person who has a sense of emotional security can share his power easily. And as he communicates this sense of security through his willingness to share his power, it helps to reassure his subordinates or group members and to develop a sense of security in them. It is important that they develop this sense of security, for without it good group feeling and morale will deteriorate.

FOOTNOTE CHAPTER 11

[1]See Albert Bandura, *Social Learning Theory*, Prentice-Hall, 1977.

Chapter Twelve

The Dilemmas of the Authority Figure Who Is Appointed

Generally speaking, there are two major ways in which an individual may become an authority figure: he is either designated by some higher authority or he is selected by the group. Professional workers attain positions of power and authority in their respective fields via a third route: by attending professional schools and securing special degrees and certificates. However, for the purpose of the present chapter, we are focusing primarily on the problems faced by the leader who works in an administrative setting.

Even in countries where the democratic tradition is the strongest, most of the individuals who function in positions of power and authority are not chosen by the persons they supervise or lead, but are selected by someone in higher authority. We are referring, of course, to individuals such as those who serve as executives in business and industry, military officers, teachers, and most government officials. Our purpose in pointing out this fact is not to imply that such a system is wrong or even that is basically undemocratic, but rather to provide a background for the discussion of problems of leadership which are likely to be faced by this large group of people. If the majority owe their position to their superiors rather than to their subordinates, then it appears that the problems we will discuss in this chapter are those that will be met in some degree by most leaders.

One of the principal difficulties encountered by appointed leaders stems from their divided responsibility. On the one hand, they have a responsibility to fulfiill toward the people they supervise and, on the other, they have a responsibility to the people who appointed them. Some of their power is derived directly from the group they supervise. If there is any doubt of this, observe the futile efforts of the appointed leader who is not accepted by his subordinates. By the simple device of withholding cooperation, they can strip him of much of his power. To be sure, he may still have the power to punish and to humiliate, but he does not have the more important power of motivating the group to do what it is supposed to do. The extent to which the appointed leader derives power from the group he supervises will therefore vary in accordance with the extent to which he is accepted by the group, as well as the extent to which he is able to help the group move in the direction of its goals and achieve its purposes.

Some of the hostility that subordinates and group members develop toward their leaders may actually be a form of jealousy, a resentment against the divided allegiance of their leader. Perhaps *they* want to be the ones to control him, or perhaps they not only want to rank first in his interests and attention but to monopolize them completely. Part of this is due to a natural desire on the part of most of us to have as much control over our fate as possible and part is due to a reluctance to accept some of the realities of our political and economic system. Hence, one of the tasks that leaders must undertake if they are to become more effective is to help subordinates and group members to accept some of these realities and to help them find and use those parts of the system that do permit freedom of expression and action.

Appointive leaders are also likely to find themselves targets for hostility because group members or subordinates see them as the representatives of the Establishment—those vague, intangible forces of authority and control, the forces who are undoubtedly responsible for all their difficulties. Thus, the high-school basketball team blame their coach and perhaps even the school administration for their defeats, ignoring the chance element that enters into any sport as well as the possibility that they may have had to play teams stronger and more skillful than they. Or perhaps some of the hostility that the stenographers display toward their bosses may be the indirect result of having to punch a time clock—just like a factory hand! To be sure, their immediate bosses may have little to say about the policy that requires clerical personnel to punch a time clock but reality is unimportant here. To the stenographers, their bosses represent management, and management is who is making them punch time clocks.

Very often appointed leaders worsen the relations with their subordinates when they overlook the fact that a major source of their power lies in their ability to motivate the people they supervise. In the final analysis, the decisions that will make group undertakings successes or failures will be made by the people who comprise the group. When an administrator ignores this basic fact and looks instead to his superiors as the main source of his power, he may be headed for frustration and failure. Actually, about all his superiors can do is to give him some legitimacy, status, and prestige by making him an administrator, or perhaps they might help him somewhat by declaring their confidence in him from time to time and by channeling expressions of organizational policy through him. But the main job of being an effective administrator, of helping subordinates to work together toward the goals selected by the organization, is up to him.

*   *   *

Probably the most difficult problems faced by any group of appointed leaders are those faced by *leaders of intermediate status*, those who directly supervise the people who do the detail work, operating equipment, or making sales. These are the leaders who are on the firing line of management, the people with heavy responsibilities, but little power and freedom—foremen, teachers, supervisors, straw bosses, scoutmasters, and the like. On the one hand, they are expected to get the job done at all costs, but on the other, they are not permitted to make decisions or changes that may be necessary to carry out their responsibilities. For example, in the situation where the stenographers feel hurt and humiliated because they have to punch time clocks, perhaps some of the bosses would like to change this policy, but being too far down the status ladder to have any effect on policy, both the bosses and the stenographers must operate within the limits of a policy set by persons on a higher level of management.

There are, of course, very good reasons why each supervisor or foreman cannot be permitted to make such changes as he feels are desirable. The granting of such freedom would interfere with the coordination and integration of various activities and functions of a large organization. However, there is an unfortunate tendency for top management in many organizations not to give foremen and supervisors enough power and enough freedom to make even low-level decisions. One of the ways that this greater freedom can be given without disturbing the coordination and stability of a large organization will be described in Chapter 14.

The intermediate leader is under strong pressure from several sides. On the one hand, he is pressured by his superiors to get the job done, to increase production, cut costs, keep the program going, and so forth. On the other hand, he feels the pressure put on him by the people he supervises to see that they are promoted, to make allowances for personal problems that interfere with their work, to see that they get the tools and supplies they are supposed to have when they need them, to see that the temperature of the working quarters is raised (or lowered), and so forth, ad infinitum. In addition to these other pressures, he has pressures of his own: a sincere desire to get the job done and keep everybody satisfied, a respect for high quality work, anxieties about being the instrument for injustice and about condoning inefficiency, and the like. Over and above this he has the same concerns about personal health and family life that everyone has, except that the intermediate leader's family life is more likely to be disturbed by his dedication to the job than is the family life of the workers he supervises. These divided loyalties are bound to come into conflict, and when an intermediate leader has to decide where his loyalties are on a given issue, he runs the risk of offending an important group of people—his subordinates, his superiors, or his family.

Most intermediate leaders resolve their conflicts in favor of their superiors. If they resolve them any other way, they run the risk of losing their jobs. If an intermediate leader is at all sensitive to the needs of the people he supervises, he will be troubled by having to make decisions against their interests and he will feel guilty at having had to let them down. In organizations where communication is easy and channels are open, intermediate leaders can get together and talk out these problems with representatives of top management as well as with the people they supervise, but where communication channels are blocked, the lot of the intermediate leader is difficult indeed.

This problem is further complicated when management violates some of the basic rules of effective leadership and makes it difficult or impossible for intermediate leaders to function adequately.

Frank Novak was the plant engineer for a factory producing solar heating systems. When the business was small, he also served as foreman, but as the volume or sales and production increased, he decided to turn his supervisory duties over to his leading workman, Carlos Jimenez. But he designated Jimenez only acting foreman, perhaps in the hope that some day he would have sufficient time to return to supervising.

The arrangement worked satisfactorily only a week, largely because Novak was busy designing a heating system to be installed in a new hospital. Once the design was finished he once again turned his attention to production and began issuing orders directly to the work force, bypassing the acting foreman. The workers were understandably upset by this turn of events. The shop steward went to top management and protested that one boss was enough and that the operatives found it impossible to work with two.

When the factory manager asked Novak what was happening, the engineer said that as far as he was concerned, the workers were a "bunch of prima donnas," and if it were up to him, he would fire the lot. When Jimenez was asked what the thought, he said frankly that he felt caught in the middle. On the one hand, he had a sense of loyalty to Novak who had taught him much of what he knew about the construction of solar heating systems and had appointed him to his present position. But on the other hand, he had a strong sense of identity with the workers, whom he had helped to train and who depended on him for help and direction. Thus he felt hemmed in and did not know which way to turn.

The manager attempted to relieve the situation by telling Novak to give Jimenez more authority. But a few days later, the workers were up in arms again. It appeared that Novak had been working with a draftsman who was preparing plans to be used by the workers. Novak told the draftsman to be sure that the drawings were clear, "because those jerks are too dumb to understand anything but the simplest forms." The draftsman repeated the comment to one of his friends in the machine shop, and a new wave of resentment rose to interfere with the production of the factory.

It seems inconceivable, at first glance, that a person holding a position of responsibility like that of plant engineer would deliberately do and say things destructive of morale and production. It is, however, possible to empathize with Novak and thus see what motivated him. Novak turned over his supervisory powers to Jimenez with considerable reluctance, because he felt he would be losing contact with important phases of the work. His anxiety about being sure that the work was being done right led him to bypass Jimenez and communicate directly with the workers. He was then humiliated when workers objected to his interference and were able to persuade top management to reduce his supervisory powers. His resentment and frustration struggled for expression, and he blurted out the unfortunate remark that was passed on to the workers by the draftsman.

Interference with the duties of foremen and other intermediate leaders is unfortunately widespread. The supervisors of intermediate leaders are human, and they sometimes forget their responsibilities, step out of their roles, and do or say things that seem insignificant at the time but that in the end undermine the authority of those below them in the chain of command.

Part of the frustration and resentment felt by Frank Novak and others in his situation is produced by the inevitable ambiguities that exist in the relationship between supervisors at various levels of organizations. It is usually difficult to state precisely where supervisory or administrative powers begin and end. The dividing line between a supervisor's power and responsibilities and those of the person next in line of authority is likely to be vague in some areas. But there is a danger in being overly specific. A division between spheres of power that is too precise promotes quibbling and interferes with communication and collaboration; if it is too vague, it leads to interference, bumbling, and poor morale. What *is* needed is mutual understanding, trust, and respect. If both the intermediate leader and his supervisor understand and trust each other, they will be able to communicate with each other, and will share responsibilities. Probably each will continue to make some errors, but their willingness to cooperate and work things out will enable them to accept and to make allowances for each other's imperfections.

Another kind of difficulty arises for the intermediate leader when top management makes demands that show no understanding of the problems he faces. Top management, for example, may insist that the company's products meet certain standards of perfection, but at the same time, foremen and supervisors may have to contend with a large turnover of employees with no adequate way to train them. If the standards are met, production goes down and spoilage goes up; if production quotas are met, standards go down. Again, communication shows up as a crucial factor. If communication is good, then it is possible for production quotas and standards to be revised to make them more realistic, or, better still, perhaps the problems of turnover and training can be solved, for they are more basic.

What very often happens in organizations where communication is not very effective is that top management will make demands without finding out whether they can be accommodated by intermediate leaders in their present work load. Perhaps the demand is for a new weekly report that takes an hour to fill out. Intermediate leaders resent this demand because they already feel overworked, because no one has explained to them why the information is important, and because they feel (probably rightly) that no one has tried to find out whether the desired information could be obtained in some other way. In the situations where communication is the poorest, the intermediate leaders are merely told to start filling out the new reports. In organizations where more attention is paid to communication, intermediate leaders are called together, the new report is described, and they are asked if they have any questions.

An even better way would be to convene the people concerned: those who need the information and the intermediate leaders who will have to supply the information. When the latter have satisfied themselves that the information is important and that they are the ones who can best supply it, they will be more inclined to be cooperative and to suggest ways in which it might be reported. It is quite possible that the group may produce a questionnaire quite similar to the one produced by the first type of organization, but the difference would be that the group-decision approach would develop a greater feeling of importance, adequacy, and involvement. Intermediate leaders who had participated in such a conference would feel that their importance to the organization had been recognized, and their morale, instead of being lowered by having to comply with the demands of an inconsiderate management, would actually be raised to a higher level.

Perhaps this approach takes a little more time initially than the other method but it saves time and money in the long run. Unfortunately, relatively few organizations conduct their internal affairs in this way. It is difficult for the leaders who constitute top management to recognize that intermediate leaders, too, are a part of management. It is difficult for them to recognize that communication is a problem, and even more difficult for them to share their power.

Unfortunately, intermediate leaders in such situations take their cues from top management. If top management hoards its power and does not permit intermediate leaders to share in decisions that affect them and their jobs, intermediate leaders will be inclined to withhold power from the people they supervise and to restrict their rights and freedoms unduly.

The climate of opinion regarding personnel practices has undergone a slow change during the last generation. In former, more authoritarian days, there was a feeling of closer identity between top management and intermediate leaders than there is today. Management was right and the worker was wrong, and the intermediate leader had no qualms about siding with the right. Today, the intermediate leader is more objective and more sympathetic to the workers' point of view than he was a generation ago, and this permits him to see matters from the viewpoint both of management and the worker. Hence the situations that appear clearcut either to the worker or to top management seem ambiguous and confused to the intermediate leader.

Mrs. Phoebe Leonard, principal of the Oceanside Elementary School, called the teachers' meeting to order.

"Before we get into the main subject for today," she said, "I would like to remind you that we are to give standardized achievement tests next Monday."

A groan went up from the assembled teachers.

"Will we have to score them again this time?" asked Miss Bandini.

Mrs. Leonard sighed. She knew that question would come up.

"I have gone over this problem with the Testing and Research Bureau of the Central Office," she said, "and I must report that they feel very strongly that teachers can learn a lot about the children they teach when they go over their achievement tests."

"I'd question that," said Miss Bandini sharply.

"I would, too," seconded Miss Partridge. "I'd like to see how much one of those psychologists from Central Office would learn about children at 2 o'clock in the morning after he had spent the entire evening scoring tests."

"I've been scoring achievement tests for my children every year for the last ten," Mrs. Hartwell chimed in, "and I find that it takes me an average of 20 to 25 minutes to do each one and to record the results. And this is when I am working right straight through, not even stopping to study the results! How they expect us to do a good job of teaching and preparation and talking to parents when we have hours and hours of test scoring to do, is more than I'll ever know."

Mrs. Leonard winced inwardly. She should have known better than to have brought up this question at the beginning of the meeting. If she didn't get them to thinking about something else, they would talk about tests for the entire forty minutes.

"I want you to know that I have told Dr. Howell at Central Office that teachers feel that having to spend extra time scoring and recording is an imposition," she broke in briskly, "and I think Dr. Howell is sympathetic, although of course he couldn't come right out and say so. And I asked whether we could get some clerical help with some of the work, but he said that the budget this year did not allow for it." She could have added that Dr. Howell was shocked at the suggestion but she felt that such a revelation would not help matters here.

"Since there does not seem to be any way that we can get out of any part of the job," she continued, "perhaps all we can do this year is to accept it and do the best we can. And now, if I may, I'd like to turn your attention to the matter of supplies. Some of you have been asking. . . ."

Mrs. Leonard sympathizes with her teachers but she can see Central Office's point of view, too. The tests are an imposition but they have to be given. It would be fairer if teachers were paid extra for the job or if there were extra clerical help available, but neither of these solutions appears to be possible. So she must insist on the job being done even though it is an imposition, even though teaching may suffer somewhat during the week that teachers are trying to get the tests scored and recorded. These are the compromises that intermediate leaders must make. Some compromises are easier to make than others, but they all involve some frustration, some anxiety, and, perhaps some guilt.

Another reason why the intermediate leader is not sure where he stands in matters that violate his sense of fairness and good human relations, is that the attitudes of top management, too, have changed in the last generation or so. Top management has more doubts today about the desirability of using drastic measures with workers. This has partly come about because workers are better organized and are better prepared to fight for their rights, partly because management is beginning to find that more humane treatment of workers gets better results and partly because the climate of public opinion regarding relations between superiors and subordinates has been undergoing a slow change in the direction of more democratic principles.

However, what has happened is that management has begun to develop ideals that are more in keeping with the principles of effective human relations (as we have described them in this book, for example), but does not know how or is not yet ready to carry them out completely. Or, to put this in another way, the leaders of top management expect intermediate leaders to behave in ways that are consistent with good human relations, but either they do not themselves observe these principles in dealing with intermediate leaders or else they insist on restrictions that make such behavior impossible. If the leaders of top management feel some guilt as a result of these inconsistencies in their behavior, it only leads them to increase the pressure on intermediate leaders and to blame them for the difficulties and failures that result from such a double standard of values.

Consequently, intermediate leaders do not know where they stand—whether they should be "tough" or "tender" with the people they supervise. On the one hand, leaders in top management tell them that the best principles of human relations require that they be tender, but on the other hand, the kinds of requirements, policies, and working conditions laid down by the leaders of top management indicate a tough policy.

Nor have the leaders of top management entirely rid themselves of the idea that intermediate leaders should be "tough" individuals, even while they endorse the principles of effective human relations. One psychologist did a research study at the behest of a large corporation, the purpose of which was to determine what kind of foremen were the most effective. When the findings rather clearly indicated that foremen who had the best production records in their departments were men who were quiet, somewhat retiring, and not very aggressive, management refused to accept the report. This did not fit in with their idea of the kind of person a foreman should be—very obviously, he should be a firm, aggressive, extraverted kind of person! The idea that an effective foreman could be any different from their stereotyped concept was completely unacceptable.

Thus the intermediate leader is enjoined to be simultaneously tough and tender; to observe the best principles of human relations but to get out the production in any case; and to do all these things in spite of the obstacles that top management has placed in his path!

*   *   *

It is little wonder that some firms and industries are finding it increasingly difficult to recruit intermediate leaders from the ranks of workers. Fewer and fewer people are willing to share the headaches and heartaches that fall to the lot of the intermediate leader. To be sure, there is the extra pay and the status but workers are more inclined these days to count the cost in anxiety. The worker of former days was more inclined to look upon promotion as a way of attaining status and of escaping from poverty. Today, workers are more adequately paid and have a better feeling of personal adequacy and status. Shorter working hours and more time for leisure have given them greater opportunity for engaging in a wider range of activities, and they are becoming increasingly reluctant to clutter up their leisure time with on-the-job worries.[1]

From the standpoint of the employed worker, the world is a much richer place today as far as intellectual, artistic, and recreational pursuits are concerned. It is easier to find freedom of self-expression through participation in a wide variety of activities. Formerly, about the only way that workers could find expression for their creative talents was to work harder, strive onward and upward, and compete with each other for promotion to positions of leadership. Today, the scope of creative experience has widened, the amount of available leisure has increased, and an ever-growing number of workers attend evening adult classes, become involved in the Parent-Teachers Association, take up hobbies, or work on constructive projects around the house.

The drawbacks of being promoted into the ranks of intermediate leaders are further highlighted by the unfortunate practice of some organizations to exploit their supervisors and foremen. Many of them do not receive extra pay for time spent on the job outside of regular working hours. To be sure, this practice is more or less traditional with managerial workers, but what often happens is that intermediate leaders have to bear the brunt of this overtime load since their responsibilities are more closely tied to the job at hand. Some organizations take advantage of their intermediate leaders merely because the latter are not organized and hence are unable to stand up for their rights. The writer knows of one foreman who left the employ of a small corporation after having been there three years. Although he was supposed to get two weeks vacation each year he had never received any. Furthermore, when he gave notice of leaving, he was made to feel that he was "letting the company down." When workers hear of such incidents, they are even more reluctant to seek or accept promotion to supervisory jobs.

Workers in many industries and localities have developed a strong sense of cohesiveness. They feel a close emotional tie with their fellow workers and are reluctant to do anything to jeopardize this relationship. Now, the worker who usually gets promoted to a position of intermediate leadership is one whose work is outstanding as compared to that of other workers or is one who tends to identify himself with the interests of management rather than that of the worker. To do either of these things means running the risk of cutting oneself off from other workers. Where cohesiveness is high and the group feeling is strong, few workers are inclined to risk "being different" in the ways we have mentioned. Being different in these ways is often regarded by workers as a kind of disloyalty to the group.

There is an increasing tendency for top management to attempt to meet the problem of recruiting intermediate leaders by bringing in people from the outside, particularly people who have special qualifications that might prove valuable if they are promoted through the ranks of intermediate leadership into positions in top management. For example, a department store recently advertised for applicants for jobs as assistant buyers, and specified that a college degree was required. The disadvantage of such a policy is that an organization may get a corps of intermediate leaders who are less attuned to the problems of the ordinary worker or group member, and the latter may feel that such supervisors do not understand their problems as well as someone who has "been through the mill." If the intermediate leaders and the workers have a marked difference in their viewpoints, it may, indeed, interfere with communication. However, merely because a supervisor happens to have been a worker at one time does not necessarily mean that his communication with his subordinates will be better than that of a supervisor who has been brought in from the outside.

As we pointed out earlier, in order for a worker to be the kind of person who comes to the attention of management as a candidate for promotion, he usually *differs* from his fellow workers both in general behavior and in viewpoint. Those who have had to work with supervisory employees promoted from the ranks know that they often have *greater difficulty* in understanding the problems of subordinates than is true with supervisors who have been brought in. Many of them do not wear authority easily, and their harsh and drastic treatment of their fellow workers creates and aggravates problems of morale and production.

What is overlooked so often is that the skills and understandings needed for effective leadership and supervision are quite different from those that go with being an efficient and productive worker. Many a person is promoted to supervisory ranks because he is an outstanding worker and because his loyalties are with management rather than with the workers. Sometimes these people turn into effective supervisory workers, but very often they do not; the average has not been as high as it would if top management had recognized the importance of human relation skills as a basic requirement of effective leadership.

*   *   *

One of the most puzzling facets to the intricate problem of improving leadership in organizations, particularly in business and industry, is the unwillingness or inability of persons in positions of power and authority to apply the findings of research in the field of human relations. One of the most notable pieces of such research was conducted at Western Electric's Hawthorne plant near Chicago in the late 1920's and early 1930's. Although its findings have been widely publicized in professional and technical journals, in textbooks, and by the popular press, many managers disregard them and try to solve problems involving human relations with the same old inefficient and unworkable solutions. The Western Electric study showed, for example, how workers' relations with their supervisors were a potent factor in the kind of attitudes they developed toward their work, and that these attitudes in turn strongly affected their efficiency and productivity. In other words, the relationship between a supervisor and an employee is a crucial one. If it suffers, morale, efficiency, and production will suffer. In spite of this fact, the top management of many organizations continues to overstress its intermediate leaders, interferes with the building of good relationships, and does not set a good example in its own relations with intermediate leaders.

In all justice, it should be noted that many of the principles of human relations we have described are contrary to popular belief. For example, studies of human relations tell us that employees improve production and efficiency (work harder) if their morale is good and if they become emotionally involved in their work as well as in the welfare of the employing organization. But popular belief tells us that people will improve production and efficiency if they can make more money thereby. If this were true, companies operating on a wage-incentive or piece-rate basis would be more productive than those in which workers are paid by the hour. But research shows that incentive methods of pay create many problems that interfere with productivity.[2] One of these problems is the tendency of workers, as we have noted previously, to set unofficial quotas that limit production even in shops that operate on a piece-rate basis.

Another reason why management is reluctant to apply principles of human relations to its dealings with workers and intermediate leaders is that the application of these principles calls for such changes as the improvement of two-way communication and the sharing of power. Such changes not only are contrary to the traditions of leadership that harken back to primitive times, but they go against the personal inclinations of those in power. It is difficult for anyone to give up anything, and persons of power and authority are no exception.

In spite of the fact that most persons in positions of power and authority consciously or unconsciously reject principles of human relations, there is a growing number of executives who are attempting to make changes in their organizations that are consonant with these principles. Sometimes these changes bring about a complete realignment of attitudes and feelings, resulting in increased morale, production, and efficiency, but more often the basic attitudes of the personnel involved are so firmly rooted in popular belief that one suspects that only lip service is being paid to the principles of human relations.

Sometimes management tries to bring about reform on a superficial level by instituting human relations courses or programs for foremen and first line supervisors but not for top management. Norman R.F. Maier, the late leader in the field of industrial psychology, said that there are three basic reasons why such programs fail. Firstly, top management executives expect supervisors to learn how to be considerate of subordinates but they themselves are not considerate of supervisors. Secondly, each supervisor tends to think of himself as a kind of exception to human relations training. *Other* supervisors probably need this training, but there is nothing wrong with *his* human relations. (This is understandable, because it is a kind of affront when someone implies that there is something wrong with our human relations; it is hard for us to accept the fact that we really could learn how to get along better with others.) Thirdly, the approaches used in these courses (lectures, formalized discussions, and films) are not ones that can change basic attitudes. If basic attitudes are unchanged, behavior will remain essentially unchanged, and any attempts to apply principles of human relations will be superficial, stilted, or insincere.[3]

The problems faced by appointive leaders of all ranks in their attempts to deal with those they supervise are intricate and involved. They will not be solved by making minor procedural changes or by trying to change the attitudes and behavior of one part of an organization without changing them in other parts. Unless leaders in key positions are willing to set the example for intermediate leaders by changing some of their basic attitudes and beliefs about workers, needed reforms in the relations between intermediate leaders and the people they supervise will not take place.

One of the ways in which changes might be initiated and both intermediate and top management leaders helped to understand, accept, and use some of the basic principles of human relations is that of the democratic group decision, a method that will be described in Chapter 14.

FOOTNOTES CHAPTER 12

[1]See C.L. Hulin and M.R. Blood, Job enlargement, individual differences, and worker responses, *Psychological Bulletin*, 1968, vol. 69, pp. 41-55.

[2]See V.H. Vroom, *Work and Motivation*, Wiley, 1964.

[3]See N.R.F. Maier, *Principles of Human Relations*, Wiley, 1952; and *Psychology in Industrial Organizations*, 4th edition, Houghton Mifflin, 1973.

CHAPTER THIRTEEN

Dilemmas of the Leader
Who Is Elected

In the last chapter we attempted to indicate how the appointed leader must contend with a handicap in the form of hostility or apathy, resulting from the fact that his subordinates have had no voice in his selection and appointment. Many appointive leaders are, of course, able to overcome the disadvantages of this handicap, but even in the best circumstances it remains a factor in the background that must continually be taken into consideration.

The questions that are before us in this chapter are whether the leader who is selected by the members of the group avoids this handicap and if, by avoiding it, whether he encounters other obstacles. We shall call this type of leader the "elected leader" to distinguish him from the "appointed leader," although many groups do not go through the formalities of an election in selecting their leaders.

There are, roughly speaking, two kinds of persons that are chosen as leaders by groups, continuing to use the term "leaders" in the broad sense as we have done throughout this book. One kind of leader is the official who is selected to represent a group, preside over it, or serve it in some other way. In this category are chairmen, legislators, moderators, county clerks, school board members, club presidents, and the like. These are people we select to serve us, because they personify in some way the qualities we associate with leadership. We select them from among ourselves, from the people we know, and, at least to the point where they begin to hold office, we regard them as "one of us." We shall have more to say on this point later.

The other kind of leader is the person who has some special training or expertness that we do not usually find among ourselves. Examples of this kind of leader are doctors, ministers, lawyers, school superintendents and judges (where they are elected), district attorneys, architects, and the like. Sometimes these people are selected by group action, such as when a congregation issues a "call" to a minister, and sometimes they are selected on a more individual basis, such as when someone chooses a lawyer to represent him in a legal matter.

The selection of a leader may be formal or informal. He may be singled out by the processes of political campaign and election or he may rise to a position of leadership because he is the kind of person to whom people turn for advice, assistance, and cousel. Most organizations and communities, large and small, have unofficial leaders of this type. Very often they do not hold positions of obvious power and importance. Sometimes they are "kingmakers" or "powers behind the throne," and sometimes they are people in minor but key positions like the woman sergeant whose help was needed to get the colonel's approval to requests in the anecdote we told about Lt. Bonesteel. Often the unofficial leader is someone who does not even have a key position, but is nevertheless a person whose judgment is trusted and whose approval must be secured if any changes in operations or procedures are to be carried out successfully.

In recent years, psychologists who have studied the "power structures" of organizations have been struck by the fact that the organizational charts which purport to show adminstrative relationships and channels of communication often do not represent an accurate picture of how business is actually conducted. In some instances, they have been able to sketch shadowy organizational charts that represent the true distribution of power behind the scenes, as it were, a chart that is quite different from the official version. The position of the sergeant we referred to above is an example of an unofficial arrangement that transcends or supersedes the officially recognized distribution of power in an Army post. Authority and power are supposed to flow from senior officers to junior officers and thence to sergeants. But Sgt. Winslow has been interposed by the tacit agreement of all persons concerned, senior and junior officers alike. They have done this because they find that the arrangement works better and because Sgt. Winslow is evidently the kind of person who fills the needs of the organization. As long as she uses her power judiciously and does not go too far in usurping the prerogatives of commissioned officers, the arrangement will function happily for all concerned. Of course, one of the disadvantages of such arrangements is that some people who find themselves in unofficial positions of power sometimes behave despotically and end up by impeding rather than facilitating the functioning of the organization.

The development of an unofficial chain of command is one of the ways that people employ in making a system of appointive leadership more democratic. It is, in effect, a subtle way of taking some of the power into their own hands. The effective leader who works in an organization that has such a dual system of control and authority will do well to acquaint himself with its operations and will work with the system rather than against it. Properly used, an unofficial system can improve communication between group members and leaders. On the other hand, attempts to destroy the unofficial system or to operate outside it may arouse anxiety and resentment on the part of group members, leading to lowered morale, production, and efficiency.

*   *   *

In the majority of instances, the elected leader usually starts out with a greater advantage in the form of good will and acceptance on the part of the group members than does the appointed leader. Because group members have shared in his selection, they feel more of a responsibility to cooperate with him. And, unless his program deviates too far from what the group already believes to be right and proper, they will be inclined to accept it as their own.

The elected leader enjoys this advantage because his followers feel that he is "one of them." Since the group participated in his elevation to a position of leadership, there is a sense of emotional investment in his success. Being able to make someone a leader gives the group a sense of power and adequacy, and they have the feeling that they not only can "make" leaders, they can also "break" them.

However, we would be somewhat less than realistic if we did not recognize the rather obvious fact that elected leaders encounter many of the same difficulties that give appointed leaders so much difficulty. They are, for example, by no means exempt from becoming the targets for hostility in its varied forms of rebelliousness, noncooperation, or apathy.

Part of the reason for this hostility apparently stems from our tendency to bracket leaders of all kinds together and to react to them as a group or a type, regardless of how they got their positions. Thus our hostile feelings toward an elected leader would be much the same as those we would have for an appointed leader, merely because they are both authority figures. This reaction generally appears after the newness of the elected leader has worn off, so to speak, as witness the less favorable attitude toward the President of the United States that traditionally sets in after his first year in office. As we mentioned previously, we are inclined to be somewhat suspicious of leaders as a group. Perhaps we forget this to some degree during the flurry of activity that surrounds their election. As we go through the preliminaries and the rituals of election, we come to feel for various reasons that perhaps *this* one is different, perhaps he really is "the ideal person." Then, after election, as this feeling of hope and expectation wears off and gives way to a more critical appraisal of the person we have elected, the faults we overlooked at first seem more glaring and we are inclined to ignore the virtues that attracted us to him in the first place. And so we find ourselves disillusioned once more, in the position of having given power to someone who is, after all, no better than ourselves.

This leads us to the question of why we selected a leader in the first place.

There are, of course, the obvious reasons that we need someone to represent us, to act on our behalf, to see that the machinery of the group operates, and to see that the goals and objectives of the group are achieved. But working cooperatively with others toward the attainment of goals is difficult, frustrating, and often unrewarding work. It involves sacrifice and self-denial, sacrifice and self-denial that are made all the more difficult when we see people who are benefiting by the group effort but are neither sacrificing nor denying themselves anything. When the trials and tribulations of working with the group wear hardest upon us, we are inclined to look for some other way, some *easier* way to attain our goals. And here is where the leader comes in.

We hope that he will lighten our burden somehow, that he will raise wages and lower prices, or keep wages down and raise prices—whatever it is that we want. Perhaps he promises us that he will do both these things, or perhaps we somehow come to believe that he will do them without his having made any promises. When the problems of life and of getting along with others become difficult, as they do at times, who can blame us for hoping that our leaders will solve them for us?

Such expectations are unrealistic, of course. The most that leaders can do is to *help* us solve our problems. This is true even when the leader is one of the professionally trained people we mentioned at the start of this chapter. A good lawyer arranges matters so that we can make proper choices, choices that are in our own best interests and in keeping with the law. A doctor prescribes drugs that keep certain infections in check so that we can recover. The clergy do not make us better people but they can help us gain a sense of participation with other religious people or can raise our normal anxieties to the point where we undertake to change our attitudes and behavior. Lawyers, doctors and the clergy do other things for us, of course, but the point is that whatever they do has the purpose and function of helping us to help ourselves.

The final responsibility for getting things done and for making necessary changes lies with groups or organizations themselves and the individuals that constitute them. We are, most of us, more or less immature and neurotic, and therefore are at times reluctant to take the responsibility and the initiative to make changes in ourselves and our environment and to do the things that need to be done. In a way, we hope when we elect or select a leader that *he* will get these things done for us, that *he* will take the responsibility or make the decision or do the work that has to be done. Hence when leaders refer responsibilities back to us or when the needed reforms and expected progress do not materialize, we are inclined to blame leaders rather than ourselves.

Some of our difficulties here are related to the fact that we have mixed feelings when it comes to being dependent on leaders. On the one hand, we would like to have leaders make decisions and do things for us, but, on the other, we resent the implication that we need or want such attention, and in a left-handed way we rather blame our leaders for making us feel dependent. Thus, if the leader does not do things for us, we feel angry because he has let us down, but if he *does* do things for us, we feel angry because it makes us feel dependent and we resent the implication that we cannot do these things for ourselves.

The experience of the Pine Cove Improvement Club serves as an example of how these principles operate.

Pine Cove is a small community with a population of two thousand or so nestled in the wooded slopes of the mountains about fifteen miles from Greater Metropole. The majority of the adults living in Pine Cove commute every day to Greater Metropole where they work as junior and semi-senior executives, as salesmen, lawyers, insurance brokers, and doctors. Sociologists would call Pine Cove an "upper-middle-class, suburban community."

The Improvement Club is one of the most active of a number of voluntary organizations which occupy the evenings and weekends of the men and women of Pine Cove. It started very informally some six years ago when a half dozen couples gathered for bridge one evening and then got to discussing whether Pine Cove should become an incorporated city. Three years later the organization had three hundred members, had outgrown two meeting-places, and was considering building a recreation center for the members and their families.

The meeting that was called to take up the proposals for building this new center was a stormy one. Trouble began when a couple of members arose and complained that the whole idea of having a center had been rushed through, and that they, having been absent from the last meeting, had not had a proper chance to voice their objections. Harold McCreary, who was presiding, got red in the face when these protests were made. He pointed out that it was no one's fault but that of the absent member if decisions were made in his absence. He also felt moved to mention the many hours spent by the Board in reviewing and preparing proposals to be presented at this meeting. And he ended by asking for a vote of confidence in himself and the Board. The vote was a resounding "Aye" and a sprinkling of "Noes," and as Harold started to go over the various proposals, several of the objectors got up and left the meeting.

Of the several plans presented to the membership, the one recommended by the Board involved the least outlay of money and the greatest expenditure of muscle power. Each family was to be asked to contribute $500 and to put in up to four hours of work per week for four months.

As the meeting wore on, the truth began to sink in that building a recrecreation center, even on a share-the-work basis, was going to be a very large undertaking, and a number of the members began to have misgivings. They raised questions as to whether the building could not be postponed till enough pledges had been collected. They asked if the estimated cost could not be trimmed down. They wondered if the members really had enough time to make the project a success. These objections called forth heated arguments from the members who had supported the proposal for a center, but no one spoke more strongly than Pete Switzer. Pete was a general contractor, somewhat older than most of the members. He had lived in Pine Cove for two years.

When Pete spoke, he expressed himself caustically about people who had no vision and were afraid to work for something that was as badly needed as the center, and he wound up his talk by offering to take personal responsibility for seeing that the center was built and built properly. The assembled group had evidently been waiting for something like Pete's speech to reassure them because a few minutes later they unanimously accepted the proposal. Howard McCreary appointed Pete Switzer to serve as chairman of the Building Committee.

As the weeks went by, the leadership of the Club began to run into difficulties that they had not anticipated. Only a hundred members made the voluntary contribution of $500, and an additional fifty gave lesser sums. However, this sum provided enough to make a down payment on the land and to lay the foundation. Pete Switzer had his architect draw up the plans and personally guaranteed the bank loan for the lot and the building, a move that he had cause to regret later. He then rounded up a committee and set them to work soliciting funds from members who had not paid the voluntary assessment. When these efforts yielded only some ten thousand dollars, Mrs. Switzer organized some of the women and held a rummage sale and some cake sales. Some of the members raised their initial contribution, a few more members sent in their assessment. However, this was all a very slow business. Pete felt that if he could start putting up a building, seeing an edifice emerge might raise the interest and optimism of the members.

It seemed to help at first. The members turned out in good force the first few Saturdays, and the framework of the building started to grow. But it became harder and harder to get help on succeeding weekends. Pete worked long hours on the project. Some weeks he spent more time working on the center than he did on his own business. Finally, after only six members showed up for a Saturday's work, he felt he had reached the end of his rope. He had advanced the project six thousand dollars from his own pocket and had signed his name to notes for twenty thousand more.

He asked to have a special meeting called to discuss the building. The president was somewhat unwilling to do so, saying that the members were getting rather tired of talking about the building, but Pete insisted. He said that it was a matter of great urgency.

The meeting was surprisingly well attended. When the president looked around the room, he decided that perhaps the membership was more interested in the building than he had assumed.

As the meeting got under way, Pete arose and told his story. He explained how he had undertaken a major share of the responsibility for building the center, but that now he was unable to continue. Not only had he obligated himself for several thousand dollars, but his own business was suffering. He proposed, therefore, that since so much of his time and money was already invested, that he take title to the center, complete it, and rent it to the membership, unless, of course, they wanted to buy it from him. He would repay the money the Club members had invested plus five thousand dollars for the time they had put into the project.

When he had finished, a storm broke over his head. It appeared that the feeling of the Club members had become increasingly bitter during the months since the decision to build the center. Some of the members resented the fact that Pete made all the decisions. Others objected to the plans that had been drawn up. Some were resentful of the fact that they had contributed money whereas others had not. Still others resented having put so much time on the building while so many of the members had stayed away. But their chief attack was focused on Pete. They implied that he had led them astray, that he had talked them into this project. They complained that he had not listened to their suggestions. And a few even hinted that Pete had figured all along that he would take over the building. Two of the members praised Pete's work and said that his offer was a generous one but their comments seemed only to highlight the angry and resentful character of the other statements. When Pete's motion finally came to a vote, it was turned down, 147 to 20.

The story has a fairly happy ending. A few days after the meeting, some of the members began to feel guilty about the way the Club had treated Pete. Furthermore, they realized that the Club could not complete the project on its own. So they worked out an arrangement whereby the City of Pine Cove would take over the project and would reimburse Pete Switzer and the Club for the money expended to date. The city drove a hard bargain, as cities sometimes do, and when it was all over, Pete found that it had cost him $2000 plus the time he had invested, and the Club was out $5000 plus the time the members had spent working on the building. However, everybody felt relieved that he had come off as well as he had, and anyway it was for the good of the community.

*   *   *

The story of Pete Switzer and the Pine Cove Improvement Club shows how well-intentioned people who are unaware of the principles of human relations sometimes work at cross purposes. The Club is happy when Pete offers to take full charge of the work because the members feel that what they need is to have someone take over the responsibility and perhaps even do the job for them. By turning over the project to Pete, they feel that they no longer have to be concerned about it—it is *his* worry, not theirs. Pete errs, too, in assuming that the way to carry out an assignment like his, one that should involve the entire membership, is to take complete charge just as he does when he is awarded a contract for a building. Consequently, he does not involve the membership in planning or in decision-making as he should. Therefore, when he comes to the members with requests for money and for time, he finds them reluctant to participate. And when the project finally comes to a halt, both Pete and the members are resentful: Pete because he feels that the members let him down, and the members because they feel that Pete let *them* down. Each blames the other for the failure of the project.

One of the things this illustrates is that some of our mixed feelings about leaders and our consequent disappointment in them stem from our inability to decide what it is we want of them. After all, what role *do* we expect a leader to play for us?

In times of crisis, it looks as though we would like a leader who is *a man on a white horse*, a leader who comes sweeping along on his charger, putting our troubles to flight. When we are anxious or frightened, a strong person, a person who is capable of vigorous, drastic action, has special appeal. Our problems are too much for us, and we want someone else to solve them.

But men on white horses have a habit of accumulating more power than we really want to give them, and they are inclined to use their power to exploit those who put them into power. Furthermore, they cannot stand to have people disagree with them. It is all or nothing with them.

If we are lucky enough to have rid ourselves of the man on the white horse, we then turn to a leader who is more neutral in character. We no longer want a man who wants a great deal of power. Now we want a leader who can get along with a minimum of power. And so we get a *caretaker* type of leader, someone who will merely keep the machinery going.

But such a leader does not have enough power to be effective. He cannot even straighten out disagreements that threaten to split us into warring camps. No, what we really need is a *harmonizer*.

So we get a leader who is skillful in adjusting differences between various groups and subgroups, someone who keeps the power of various factions in a state of balance. But the trouble now is that we are not making enough progress. There are projects to be undertaken, things that need doing. But our harmonizer-leader will not start us on doing them until he has made sure that there is no opposition to the proposed projects. The difficulty is that there is always somebody opposed to something, and while we are waiting around to see that everyone is satisfied, we could have completed the project and be reaping its benefits! No, the harmonizing leader leaves something to be desired, too.

Evidently, the kind of leader we need is an *aggressive doer*, someone who knows how to get things going and carry them through to completion. Someone who can manage us and get out of us the best that is in us. But the trouble now is that after a while, we wonder where we are going. We are travelling along at a great pace and working our heads off, but are we getting to where we really want to go? We wonder if change and the completion of projects are really progress. What does it all mean? Are we any happier, any more adequate because of it?

And so we get a *reassuring leader,* one who gives us emotional support, who makes us feel adequate and secure. Yet this, too, begins to pall after while. We want more than comfort, we want to do things for ourselves, we want to look reality in the face. . . .

These are a few of the many roles we expect leaders to take. If we expect any one leader to take all these roles, we are obviously expecting too much of him. Given our expectations, it is amazing that so many leaders do so well.

Perhaps the key dilemma in these conflicting expectations that we have for the leaders we select is that we expect them to be both our servants and our masters. We want them to lead us but we also want them to follow our lead. And when both we and our leaders become confused at times because of these diametrically opposed expectations, misunderstanding and resentment is the inevitable result. Very often leaders can use disagreements as an entering wedge for improving communication because at such times they can more easily command the attention of those they serve and lead. Other leaders are less adequate to the demands of their ambiguous situation and become the casualties of the democratic process.

Another difficulty centers around power. Do we give our leaders enough power? Or do we give them too much? Or do we give them any power at all? Perhaps we *give* them power, *lend* them power, and *deny* them power all at once. The human race has had such a long history of being taken in by leaders, yet leaders certainly need some power if they are to do the minimum that is expected of them. We have not resolved these issues satisfactorily. Consequently we criticize our elected leaders at times for taking too much power and sometimes we criticize them for not making effective use of the power we think we have given them.

*   *   *

Every so often we read in the public press of the shortage of leaders. Each individual who writes such articles or issues such statements undoubtedly has a different thing in mind, but it is also quite possible that in some respects they are all writing about the same thing. In other words, one person may be concerned about what he thinks is the low caliber of person we are getting in public office; another may be saying in effect that we do not have a person of adequate stature to oppose the party in power in the race for mayor; and another may have reference to the difficulty of finding intermediate leaders for business, industry, and government service. But underlying each of these complaints may be an awareness that people who are potential leaders are reluctant to expose themselves to the demands, responsibilities, and anxieties that go with leadership.

The problem faced by some voluntary organizations is a case in point. Many of these groups experience a great deal of difficulty in getting people to serve as officials because the member who runs for office knows that he will have difficulty in getting other members to cooperate and to work for the program of the group, and that he may end up by doing most of the work himself. He knows, too, that if he makes all the decisions and does all the work, group members will resent this. On the other hand, if the decisions are not made and the work is not done, group members will feel that he has let them down. And so, when the time comes to elect officers, potential candidates run for cover, as it were, and try to think of all the reasons why they should not be placed on the ballot.

However, perhaps we are being too critical. One of the outstanding characteristics of American life is the thousands upon thousands of voluntary organizations that serve our social, recreational, professional, and intellectual needs. Probably no other country on earth provides such a rich variety of voluntary organizations for the participation of its citizens. The typical American with a professional status or a position of some importance belongs to several of these groups simultaneously. Consequently, he feels pulled in several ways at once, and when his name comes up for president of the Sunnyside Improvement Club, he remembers that he is already the chairman of the Membership Committee of his professional organization, on the Board of Directors of the church, a scoutleader, and actively interested in a service club. Under such circumstances, we cannot blame him for feeling harried and for urging that someone else be nominated. The only difficulty is that the other people who are likely candidates are in the same fix.

The solution to this dilemma is a two-fold one. Most of the offices in most organizations are held by a minority of the members, the majority being unwilling or unable to make the emotional investment that would prepare them for positions of leadership. Perhaps it is the fear of being elected to a position of responsibility that keeps some of them from involving themselves more deeply. What is needed here is an honest facing of the problem by the members of these organizations, coupled with long-range programs aimed at spreading participation more completely throughout the membership.

The other part of the solution—and this is as difficult and tedious as the first part—involves getting more people to participate in voluntary organizations. Studies that have been made of such participation show that it is largely concentrated in the college-educated, middle-class portion of the population. White-collar folk are much more likely to join voluntary groups than are blue-collar people.[1] There seems to be no easy way to get blue-collar people to increase their participation in voluntary groups. Often they have the feeling that they are not wanted, and it is very likely that this feeling has some basis in fact. Any attempt to enlist the participation of this segment of the community will have to be done carefully and with great sensitivity on the part of the sponsors so as to avoid situations which may humiliate or offend the persons they are trying to recruit.

Neither of these solutions is an easy one, yet both are worthwhile. If leadership can be shared on a broader basis in organizations and if such organizations come to represent more of their communities than they do at present, the cause of community solidarity and general public morale will be greatly advanced. One of the main reasons why leaders must contend so often with hostility is that leadership and its responsibilities are not shared on a wide enough basis. If more people could be encouraged to share in the leadership of voluntary organizations, the decades ahead should see the growth of greater cooperation between leaders and group members not only in voluntary organizations but also in employment situations and elsewhere in our national life.

This is not to imply that we are not making progress toward these goals. The continuing rise in the educational level of our citizens, the growing size of the middle class, and the lowering of class, ethnic, and sex barriers is making it possible for larger segments of the population to participate in the kinds of community activities we have described. But the progress is spotty; it is much better in some communities than in others, and not nearly enough people grasp the importance of broadening the base of participation in voluntary groups. As a result, there are large segments of the population who remain on the outside of this vital area of our community life. This fact not only underlies the active and passive hostility with which leaders must contend, but it is probably related to the apathy and ignorance regarding national and international affairs that come to public attention from time to time. People who have had no experience in sharing the power and responsibility of leadership are less likely to be interested in electing leaders to represent them in local, state, and national government, and are even less likely to take a hand in shaping the course of international affairs.

FOOTNOTE CHAPTER 13
_____

[1]See G.A. Almond and S. Verba, *The Civic Culture: Political Attitudes in Five Nations,* Princeton University Press, 1963.

CHAPTER FOURTEEN

How Authority Figures Can Increase Their Effectiveness by Sharing Power

Throughout the industrialized world, and especially in North America, a new pattern of leadership has been emerging over the last few centuries. It is a pattern that is increasingly democratic, one that relies less on the concentration of power in the hands of a few and more on the participation of all. The relatively recent appearance of dictatorships in developing countries may appear to be an exception to this trend, but when we compare these governments to the absolute despotisms that prevailed in these areas a century or two ago, it is clear that the trend toward greater participation and the sharing of power has penetrated there as well.

It is therefore safe to say that we are in the midst of what has been and what promises to be a long, drawn-out process of transition, whereby older, more traditional patterns of leadership and authority become converted to ones that are more democratic. In some instances, the right to share power was won through force of arms, but it more usually resulted from argument, persuasion, and the dissemination of ideas, values, and social norms.

During the earlier stages of this process of transition, people thought that the application of democratic principles was limited to politics and the administration of self-government organizations. If they applied to employment situations, it was felt that it was only in a very limited sense. And most people believed that democratic principles had little relevance to family life, where the father was lord and master, and the mother was a junior partner in power.

Our thinking about these matters has changed markedly in the last century or so. First unions, and then government regulations, have forced limitations on employers' powers, and the powers of parents have likewise become subject to legal restrictions. The most significant agent of change, however, has been the seepage of democratic values from the public to the private area of human experience. Although we may try to

153

compartmentalize our lives, the values and attitudes that we employ in one field have a way of influencing our behavior in other areas. For example, when we as a people concluded that men had equal political rights, we did not think that this principle also applied to women. It was not until two generations ago that we admitted our error and added the necessary amendment to the Federal Constitution. Many of us still have not completely accepted this principle, for women do not yet have full and equal rights. For example, they get less pay for equal work and they are still underrepresented in high-status occupations and in elective offices.

For a long time it was difficult to see why the relations between employers and employees should be based on democratic principles. It seemed much simpler and more appropriate to pattern the structure of business and industry after the family, with the owner or manager playing the role of the father and the employees playing the role of his children. However, the strong ties and loyalties of the family seemed out of place in the employment situation, and employees not only were not children, they resented being treated as children.

On the other hand, there was the matter of elections. Democracy and elections were intimately associated in our minds. We favored free elections for aldermen and congressmen but we could not see how working situations would be improved if workers elected foremen and managers. So, instead, we developed the ideas that democracy in employment meant that workers could quit one employer and go to work for another, that they could form unions, and that they could strike. These rights gave workers more freedom and power and brought democracy to the employment situation in a limited sense. They protected the worker against some forms of coercion and exploitation but they often tended to drive wedges between employers and workers, whereas the basic arrangement that makes business and industry function successfully is one of collaboration and cooperation. Furthermore, a great many leaders of business and industry resented the growing power and freedom of the worker because they realized that their control over him was thereby weakened. The best way to be assured of the production of a worker, they felt, was to control him. But the idea of control seems opposed to democratic ideals.

One way to look at this dilemma is to analyze it in terms of "power" and "love." By "power," using the word as we have previously, we mean the ability to control people. Two of the commonest forms of power are wealth and authority. Through the use of money, a form of wealth, we can persuade people to do what we want them to do. This is a kind of power-sharing, although when we as employers pay people to do things for us, it is because we expect to turn their labor into profits, so that we end up with more money or power than we started with. When we use the power of authority, we get people to do what we want them to do by presenting them with a choiceless situation or rather a choice between punishment and no punishment. Love provides quite a different motivation. We are of course using "love" in its broadest sense, encompassing the concepts of altruism, acceptance of and respect for others as individuals and fellow human beings, and brother/sisterhood. We all have a basic need to love and be loved, a need that underlies all positive forms of human interaction. It provides the "social cement" that unifies all humanity.

In the traditional family, authoritarian and autocratic as it was, both power and love played an important part. Children submitted to the power of their elders, but it was the love they received and felt for their parents and each other that made life worth living. A similar situation obtains with respect to the autocratic and authoritarian leader. Some of the hold that such a leader has over his followers is due to power but much of it lies in his ability to inspire loyalty and to make his followers feel that he has their interests at heart.

To a large degree, the development of a democratic pattern for living was a reaction against the older, more authoritarian patterns. Many of our forebears were suspicious of the emotional relationship that existed between authoritarian leaders and their followers because they felt that it blinded the followers to the evils of the system that held them captives. Consequently the system they worked out is concerned largely with equalizing power and thus providing for freedom. The citizen was expected to feel loyalty to the state, of course, because that was to his advantage and in his best interests, but personal loyalty to a single leader was dangerous because it might lead to the development of an aristocracy and the downfall of the republic.

As the democratic pattern emerged, one of the devices that we developed as a means of equalizing power was the direct ballot. We have never completely lost our fear of dictatorship and have therefore defended and maintained our system of free elections as a defense against this possibility. Our concern about maintaining the integrity of the ballot helped reinforce the idea in our minds that the essence of democracy lay in the secret ballot rather than in the basic and intrinsic worth (hence the equality) of each individual in every aspect of life.

The Western Electric study we referred to in the last chapter helped to bring the relationship of democracy to the employment situation into better focus. What the researchers found was that we had been overlooking an important force in the lives of workers. They found that what we have referred to as the "love" relationship played a crucial part in the development of satisfactory relationships between management and employees. Workers demonstrated in several ways that being regarded by one's immediate supervisor as an important person was an essential part of being an effective employee. In a series of experiments on working conditions, the reachers showed that developing a feeling of group pride and loyalty resulted in production far beyond the expectations of company experts. They also discovered that the ability to have confidential communication in a free and comfortable atmosphere with company representatives improved the morale and the attitudes of workers toward their work.

During the ensuing years, psychologists and sociologists have been conducting an increasing number of studies which confirm the findings of the Western Electric study. These studies show, generally speaking, that when business and industry operate on a power-oriented basis, morale, production, and efficiency are lower than when operations are on a love-oriented basis. In other words, when workers feel that their importance as individuals is recognized and accepted, they respond by increasing their effectiveness.

As we have pointed out elsewhere, there has been a general reluctance on the part of management to accept the findings of this research just as there has been a general inability to see how the basic principles of democracy apply to the employment situation. Nevertheless, an increasing number of leaders in business and industry are becoming aware that something essential is lacking when relationships between employers and employees are maintained on solely a power basis. Hence, there has been a rediscovery, so to speak, of the importance of the love factor in human relationships. To put this a little differently, we are beginning to realize that the relationship between employer and employee should be a *human* relationship rather than a *power* relationship and that emotional factors are at least as important as economic factors. Probably even more important.

Many of the initial efforts to "humanize" employer-employee relationships were unsuccessful. Sometimes they failed because management did not realize that workers must participate in bringing about changes if the latter are to be wholly accepted. Hence, instituting profit-sharing plans, putting paper towels in the washroom, and building bowling alleys have often failed to produce dividends in the shape of better moral and higher production. At other times, moves on the part of the management to improve a power-heavy situation have been mis-understood by workers, by union leaders, or even by some of the people entrusted with carrying out the plans. To give due credit to the leaders of management, they have not stopped trying to humanize their relations with employees. Even though real successes have been limited to a small proportion of business establishments, each year sees a growing number of organizations becoming actively interested in programs designed to improve human relations.

*   *   *

It may be well at this point to go over some of the chief reasons why managers need to develop a different approach in dealing with their subordinates or group members.

The following points seem to be basic to any enlightened relationship between an authority figure and a subordinate or group member:

1. The subordinate or group member must be helped to develop a deeper sense of personally participating or sharing in what the group or organization is trying to accomplish.

2. Both authority figures and subordinates (or group members) must work together to see that there is a reasonable balance of security and freedom—security against unreasonable and unwarranted attack or reprisal from the other, and freedom to enjoy basic human rights and to develop one's best potentials.

3. Authority figures need to be scrupulous in seeing that the channels of communication are open and operating.

4. Authority figures must develop an emotional climate that promotes morale and good group feeling or cohesiveness.

Implicit in these four points is the idea that authority figures must learn to share power and to provide opportunities for subordinates and group members to participate in making decisions about problems in which they are involved. Employees are less likely to feel a sense of identity and responsibility toward the organization that employs them if they never get an opportunity to express their attitudes and ideas about significant aspects of their work. Management cannot continue to monopolize decision-making without giving workers the feeling that management thinks they are not important or intelligent or good enough to have ideas of their own.

Power- and decision-sharing are both means and ends. They are the means of reassuring subordinates and group members that their leaders regard them as important people, people who "count," people who are entitled to a fair share in matters that affect their welfare. Not only does such a gesture reassure but it arouses reciprocal feelings—the subordinate or group member says to himself in effect: "If my leaders have confidence in me and are willing to trust me, I can certainly develop trust and confidence in them, and it will not be necessary for me to think of ways to outwit and trick them or to get back at them."

Each of the points we mentioned is interdependent. Unless authority figures can assure subordinates and group members that conditions of security and freedom exist, there will be no free communication. Free communication is essential to morale and cohesiveness, and both morale and cohesiveness are basic to developing a deeper sense of participation in the group or organization.

*   *   *

If a new approach is to make any real changes in the relationship existing between leaders and their subordinates or group members, it must open up new channels of communication and must demonstrate a willingness on the part of leaders to share the power to make decisions. Furthermore, it must stimulate subordinates and group members to a greater awareness of their importance to the organization and the organization's importance to them. Let us examine some of the techniques and methods that various groups and organizations are employing in their attempts to humanize their operations.

The *suggestion box* is a device that is sometimes used as a means of providing employees with a way of making anonymous complaints about working conditions. The use of a suggestion box usually indicates that the leaders of management are aware that effective two-way communication does not exist and that they are looking for some of the reasons why morale and production are not as high as they should be. The suggestion box, theoretically at least, gives the worker some feeling of freedom and security, because he can make his complaint anonymously, without fear of reprisal. However, whether he will do so depends on whether he believes that management is really interested in finding out what he thinks and, more important, whether management will really do anything about his complaint. Another disadvantage is that written communication is a poor substitute for oral communication. Many workers do not like to write and feel uncomfortable and embarrassed about putting things in writing. This is true even for a great many people who have gone to high school and beyond. Furthermore, written communication does not provide the opportunity to come to the understanding that is possible in the give-and-take of conversation.

The extent to which suggestion boxes will succeed in improving a situation will depend to a large extent on whether the group and its leaders take them seriously. Very often they start off well, but when management makes no formal reply to the suggestions put into the box and when no reforms are forthcoming, employees come to regard the device as just another insincere gesture. Even at best, suggestion boxes are regarded with some suspicion. The *New Yorker* once published a cartoon showing an executive going through a stack of papers from a suggestion box with a fingerprint detection kit and a file of fingerprint records at his elbow. What gives such a cartoon its special point is that it reflects what a lot of people have thought all along about suggestion boxes and the motives of people who put them there.

Studies and surveys of morale are often used as ways of finding out what subordinates and group members think of the organization, its goals and objectives, working conditions, and management. The use of such devices also indicates an awareness on the part of leaders that morale *is* a problem and that existing lines and methods of communication are not producing desired information. Morale surveys also preserve the anonymity of the employee by using anonymous questionnaires or "tear ballots" (which can be answered by making small tears at various places, thus making it unnecessary to use pencils).

If such surveys are conducted by people who understand the technical problems of constructing questionnaires, writing proper instructions, and interpreting the results, a great deal of valuable information can be gathered together and reported in ways that can be easily and quickly comprehended. If a morale survey is expertly done and properly reported, it may be possible for management to tell almost at a glance what the chief problems in the organization are.

However, there are several shortcomings. Employees do not necessarily feel, just because they have filled out a questionnaire, that they have really communicated with management or that they have actually participated in decision-making. After all, a questionnaire provides a remote and impersonal means of communication. Furthermore, the questions that are listed on a questionnaire may not cover the chief matters that are bothering the workers. Another point is that management does not usually share the information it receives from its questionnaires. A morale survey is all too often conducted for the sole benefit of management who is free to accept it or ignore it at will.

Some of the disadvantages of the questionnaire method may be overcome by the use of *open-end interviews*, whereby trained interviewers (usually brought in from the outside) ask workers questions that are to be answered in the workers' own words. Such methods avoid the danger of putting answers in workers' mouths and thus biasing the results. They have the further advantage of providing clues that aid in interpreting the real attitudes of employees. Furthermore, since employees get a chance to talk and to express themselves fully, they have the feeling of communicating to someone who will carry their message to management.

The opportunity to communicate through self-expression is also one of the chief advantages of *personal counseling* (or personnel counseling). Personal counselors are trained psychologists who are available to talk with employees who want to discuss problems of any type in a confidential setting. The Western Electric Company was the first organization to use this technique on a large-scale basis when it hired a group of college graduates, trained them in interviewing techniques, and gave them the broad assignment of talking to employees with a view to finding out what their problems were, working with supervisors on developing better methods of supervision, and improving communication generally within the company. As the interviewers undertook this project, they discovered that a valuable by-product of their activities was the improvement in attitudes and feelings experienced by the people who came to see them about their problems. In many cases, the interviewers, merely by being interested and sympathetic listeners, were able to help in a psychotherapeutic way to relieve anxiety and reduce hostility.

Personal counseling is a particularly helpful approach to improving human relations because it enables the worker to initiate communication which, if he wishes, will eventually reach persons in management who can do something about his problems. This gives him the feeling of being able to influence decisions, at least indirectly. Furthermore, it provides an opportunity for him to get a great deal of hostility and resentment off his chest in a harmless way. Since the personal counselor must treat all such communication as confidential, the worker feels a great deal of freedom in saying what he thinks, and the fact that management has made it possible for him to use the services of such a counselor is visible evidence that management wants to communicate with him and is not afraid of having him express his hostility. People who have to go around with hostilities and bad feelings bottled up inside have difficulty in serving as effective employees or group members. Having a great deal of unexpressed hostility usually has the effect of reducing efficiency and production and interferes with cooperation and the development of good group feeling. By giving such workers a chance to talk through their problems and to reexamine and reappraise them, management helps to remove or reduce this threat to morale.

One of the shortcomings of personal counseling as an approach to improving human relations is that its initial cost is expensive, although long-range dividends make the initial cost worthwhile. It is a slow method because it takes time to talk to people and it takes time for the benefits to filter through the group and change their attitudes. Furthermore, it does not involve enough of the key people whose attitudes need to be changed if the human relations in the organization are to be placed on a sounder footing. As we have said earlier, it does little good to improve the human relations at the lower levels of an organization when no real changes are taking place among the leadership. Another disadvantage to this method is that communication between the employee and top management is filtered though the personal counselor and perhaps through several intermediate executives before it reaches the person who can *really* make decisions.

The problem of improving morale and communication is only *partly* a problem involving individuals. It is to a much greater extent a problem that concerns *groups* of people simultaneously at various levels of power and authority. What we need, therefore, is a method that will give people from various administrative ranks opportunities to interact and to communicate with each other directly in a group setting. Such a method, if used extensively, could be the major technique in a program designed to improve morale and communication.

The approaches we have described are consistent with the views of Rensis Likert, views that have, incidentally, strongly influenced the thinking expressed throughout this book. Likert[1] says that management practices have, over the ages, gone through four major stages or systems. System I, the most primitive, is what might be termed the "carrot-and-stick" approach, whereby subordinates are either rewarded for satisfactory performance or punished for unsatisfactory performance. In actual practice, System I is characterized by a great deal more "stick" than "carrot," because administrators have an all-too-human tendency to take

satisfactory performance for granted and seem interested only in repri-
manding or punishing subordinates when their behavior does not come up
to expectations.

System II is more benevolent than System I, in that rewards are
emphasized more than punishments. Like System I, however, it regards
subordinates as anonymous cogs in the production machinery, whose
satisfactory operation depends only on whether the right levers are pressed
or the right switches are pulled. System II's counterpart in the
psychological laboratory is B.F. Skinner's[2] operant-conditioning strategy,
whereby subjects — rats, pigeons, or humans — are taught to behave
properly by having their responses positively reinforced or "shaped" by an
experimenter.

System III is even more benevolent than System II. Although the control
of the organization remains firmly in the manager's hands, subordinates
initiative is encouraged, and there is some sharing of responsibility.
Workers are thus treated more like individuals and less like faceless
automatons.

Under System IV, the manager takes the initiative to see that
responsibility and authority are shared throughout the organization by
means of group problem solving and group decision making. System IV is,
according to Likert, the ideal approach available to organizations that
have to cope with changing conditions.

Organizations can translate System IV's philosophy into operational
terms by structuring decision-making processes according to what Likert
calls the "linking-pin" theory or principle. In organizations structured
according to this model, supervisors and workers are grouped in
"families" that are bound together through their common members, who
serve as linking pins. Each organizational family is composed of a
supervisor and the individuals who report to that supervisor. The family
assumes responsibility for its work as a total group and arrives at group
decisions regarding its tasks. The leader of each group, in turn, serves as a
member of another organizational family, thus linking it to the leader's
"home"family. In other words, each family leader serves not only as the
head of a group but also holds membership in a group of peers who meet
with their own leader.

The linking-pin arrangement is designed to facilitate communication
throughout the organization by encouraging self-expression, feedback,
and the sharing of power and responsibility.

*   *   *

The late Norman R.F. Maier[3], who was a prominent leader in
humanistic methods in management, said that he approved of Likert's
approach, but felt that it did not go far enough in stressing the group-

decision method, which Maier believed provided the most practical avenue to the sharing of power and responsibility in organizations.

He said that it was important to note that the group-decision method should not be confused with popular ideas of democracy which stress the majority-rule ethic or foster leaderless "laissez-faire" conditions that lead to anarchy and chaos. Unlike laissez-faire, Maier's group-decision approach has a definite structure: a leader poses a problem to a group and leads a discussion that enables members to reach a decision. It is essential, of course, that members of the group understand the problem and have a personal interest in it.

Maier suggested a four-step approach in the decision-making process, but also noted that the steps need not be carried out in the order listed below.

The first step is that of *studying the problem.* The leader determines his responsibility and the responsibility of his group to the problem concerned. Do they have sufficient administrative freedom to handle the problem or will it be necessary to consult other groups or administrators? He analyzes the situation to determine whether existing regulations require that the problem be solved in a certain way and whether the problem is one that actually interests the group. If the group is indifferent to a problem, they will not concern themselves with solving it. On the other hand, it may be necessary to submit a problem to the group to find out whether it is one that they view as important to them. Then there are problems that members do not view as important but which really have a long-range effect on their welfare. It may be necessary for the leader to show them how it *does* affect them and perhaps raise their "normal anxiety" a bit.

At this first stage it is also important for the leader to check his own attitude toward the proposed method of solving the problem at hand. Is he really ready to have them look at the long-range aspects of the problem? Or does he want only that they come to a solution which applies to the immediate situation? Is he willing to deal with participants on a man-to-man basis, respecting the views of each person and avoiding paternalism? Does he believe that the group is capable of solving the problem? Is he willing to live with the solution they agree on? In other words, is he willing to accept their solution even though it is different from the one he has in mind?

During the first stage, the leader should plan his presentation of the problem. He should be able to show the group why it *is* a problem. He should focus it on the real issues. For example, if the problem concerns the tardiness of a few employees, whose production is normal, it would be unreasonable to give production as a reason for concern. Perhaps the leader is really concerned about the effect their tardiness has on other groups. If so, he should be honest in expressing this concern. It may be added parenthetically that if the leader gives the problem an incorrect or inappropriate focus, the group will often supply the correction.

The second step or stage is that of *sharing the problem*. It helps if the problem is presented in positive terms rather than stating it as an implied criticism that puts the group on the defensive to begin with. As Maier suggested, "How can we improve our job so that we get a better start in the morning?" is better than "What can we do about tardiness?" Problems should be stated in ways that indicate why the problem should be a matter for group concern and that stimulate interest in solving the problem. It is often very helpful if the problem is stated in terms of the nature of the situation in which the group works. For example: "Because our largest volume of business comes during the noon hours when some of the staff are out to lunch, we have more than we can handle at some times of the day and not enough to do at others." The problem may also be presented in terms of fairness to all concerned, such as: "How can we solve the lunch-hour problem in a way that will be fair to everyone?"

During this stage it is important to have all the necessary facts at hand. In the lunch-hour situation mentioned just above, the leader should have a record of the number of calls for service received at various hours during the day. These facts should be presented briefly at the start of the meeting and not brought out later to prove that somebody is wrong. Maier suggested that if a solution is proposed that is not feasible because of certain facts that the leader accidentally omitted, the solution should be listed with the other proposals, and the group encouraged to search for other possibilities, or else the leader should frankly admit that he forgot to mention certain essential facts. Maier also points out that a leader does not lose face if he has to get certain facts from his superiors during the course of a meeting.

It is very useful to have a blackboard during this and other stages of the meeting. Listing proposals, as well as their advantages and disadvantages, is very helpful. This technique enables the group to evaluate and compare proposals and to return to ideas that came up earlier in the discussion. Not only that; the very act of seeing the leader write down an idea contributed by a group member goes a long way with group members in demonstrating that the leader is willing to accept each member's contribution on an equal basis and is interested in seeing that everyone gets a fair hearing.

The third step is *discussing the problem*. The leader's role here is to encourage free discusson and to make it possible for everyone to participate who wants to, without necessarily putting pressure on members who are reticent. Some members will be more timid than others but will indicate their desire to participate by leaning forward or by opening their mouths slightly when someone is making a point. The leader should be alert to pick up such signs, and when the other member has finished, he should make it a little easier for the shyer member to enter the discussion by suggesting: "Did you want to make a point, Kimberley?" or by asking some such appropriate question.

Of basic importance at this and other stages of the discussion is the maintenance of a friendly, relaxed atmosphere. Each member should feel perfectly free to say what is on his mind without fear of criticism or reprisal. Dr. Maier points out that a raised eyebrow, a sharp glance, or any other expression of blame or doubt on the part of the leader can destroy this friendly atmosphere.

The group should do most of the talking and answering of each other. Many questions directed at the leader can be turned back to the group by the leader's asking: "What do the rest of you think about this idea?" or "I'm very interested in hearing how some of the other people here feel about this very important issue," or the like. When a discussion is going well, group members will be directing questions and answers back and forth among themselves rather than at the leader. The leader should avoid stepping into a discussion and commenting on some idea that seems weak and impractical to him; if there are weaknesses in the idea, it is much better for the group to discover them. Leaders will probably have misgivings on this point, but if they stay with the rules and permit the group to struggle with the problem, they will almost invariably be amazed at the ability of the group to come out with workable and sensible solutions.

The leader can be of great assistance during this stage by helping the group to stay with the problem instead of wandering off on irrelevant tangents. At such times he can ask: "Should we stay with the problem we started out with—or shall we follow through on this interesting idea we have been talking about for the last few minutes?" Usually the group will come back to the main problem, but if it does not, the leader should go along with the group. It may be that the new problem *is* more important. However, under such circumstances, it is legitimate to ask toward the end of the discussion: "We have five minutes left; what shall we do about the problem we started with? Shall we postpone decision till our next get-together? Shall we decide now on one of the several solutions presented?"

Some groups are more inclined than others to wander from the subject, and the leader may have to ask several times during the course of a meeting: "Is this idea one that we should take up at another meeting?" or "Is there any way we can work Frank's idea into the solution of the main problem before us?" If he asks these questions in a kindly, thoughtful way, in the spirit of one who is genuinely interested in *helping the group solve the problem*, he is not likely to give offense or to spoil the friendly atmosphere of free discussion.

If certain members tend to dominate the discussion, the leader may have to direct some questions to more reticent members. He might say: "It is very important that any decision we make should reflect the views of all of us. I wonder if anyone else would like to comment on the problem or the solutions we have here on the blackboard." If this does not call forth comment from the quieter members, he might say: "William, you have been here longer than any of us (or, you have had a lot of experience with this problem); what do you think about it?" If William says that he would rather listen than talk, he should not be pressed.

One of the important functions of the leader during this stage and others is to respect and protect "minority opinions." People who disagree with the majority of the group often hold back unless they get some encouragement or are assured that they will not be rejected personally because their opinions happen to differ from those of the rest of the group. The leader can help out here by saying: "Let's get your suggestion down on the blackboard, Joe, so we can see what it looks like," or "The point you raise gives us a new angle, Harry."

Sometimes the minority opinion is the solution that wins out with the group; the group may be so wrought up about some real or fancied injustice that they may overlook certain important aspects of the problem until the comment of one or two members brings them to the attention of the entire group. When leaders accept minority opinions at face value, their proponents are less likely to feel that they should defend their position.

Minority opinions are sometimes charged with hostility, and the expression of that hostility helps to provide relief. The leader can help out here by saying, as Maier suggested: "That's what we are here for—to find out how we feel about this situation," or "Jim's point shows that we have different ideas on the question, which is all to the good. After all, we are here to work out differences."

The fourth and final step is *solving the problem*. The solution, according to Maier, is really a meeting of the minds. It will contain part of the thinking of all members of the group. It should not be necessary to vote. Voting introduces an element of power that tends to divide people rather than to bring them together. The best solutions are those that are accepted unanimously. If there are two or three dissenting voices, it may even be desirable to postpone the final decision for a meeting or two until the entire group can accept the solution or arrive at another. If it is necessary to act immediately, and it is not always as necessary as we like to think, sometimes the leader can ask the dissenting members whether they are willing to accept the majority proposal on a trial basis. Some sincere attempt should be made to reconcile differences. Or, sometimes, he can meet with them privately and give them a chance to talk out what it is that is troubling them about the solution.

An important function of the group leader is that of summarizing and checking for group agreement. As he senses that the group has reached a conclusion, he should ask, "Am I correct in saying that this is the feeling of the group?" or "Am I giving this its proper interpretation?" Summarizing and checking helps the group to decide whether it really wants the solution they have tacitly accepted and shows who is for or against the solution. This gives minority viewpoints that have not been heard a chance to have an airing.

The solution accepted by the group should specify how and when it is to be done. Sometimes groups decide on the *what* of a solution, but because they overlook the need to agree on a *how* and a *when*, misunderstandings and disagreements develop. It occasionally happens that considering the *how* and *when* will show the solution to be unworkable or unacceptable because the group was not realistic in its approach to the problem. If this occurs, the group should be given a chance to reconsider the problem.

Indeed, the leader should be willing to reopen the question at the request of the group or if he senses that the group wants to reconsider, even though he would prefer that the group would take less time to make up its mind. If he really trusts the group, and such an attitude on his part is essential if this method is to work, and he is less likely to think poorly of the group for not having hit the ideal solution on its first try. Sometimes it will be necessary for the group to examine a less adequate solution, only to find that it really does not solve the problem, whereupon the problem must be brought up again at a later meeting. By demonstrating his willingness to let the group solve the problem in its own way, the leader reaffirms his confidence in the group members to make decisions and to make wise use of the power he has shared with them.

*   *   *

Maier's approach resembles, in a number of ways, a group-decision method employed by Japanese manufacturers, whose ability in recent years to dominate the international market for automobiles, cameras, and electronic equipment has amazed the world. What has made Japanese products especially attractive is their high quality. This is in marked contrast to their pre-World War II output, which was notorious for its shoddiness.

The problem of product quality was attacked by the Japanese in the following manner. In the early 1950's, they decided that the best approach to the manufacture of high-quality products, and thus building up their export trade, was that of locating and correcting flaws in materials and production processes in order to forestall the appearance of defects in the final product. This contrasts to the practice usually followed in Western industry—that of depending on end-product inspection as a means of quality control.

The task of implementing this basic decision was entrusted to "quality-control (QC) circles," each composed of about ten workers and a foreman, who meet several times a month to find solutions to production problems in their area. These QC circles are expected to arrive at unanimous decisions, an approach quite different from that usually employed in American industry, where an adversary approach is preferred. (Under an adversary approach, two or more factions argue in favor of a favored solution; the group making the best presentation wins the argument and, presumably, has its solution accepted by the group or by management.)

The process embodied in QC circles fit in very well with the family-centered culture that characterizes Japan; the company is viewed as a life-long extension of the family, so that workers feel no conflict in loyalties in collaborating with management. American workers, on the contrary, are more guarded in their relations with their supervisors, feeling that if they overcommit themselves, management will take advantage of them.

The Japanese practice requires that major decisions in industry (as well as in government) be reached only after extensive consultations with all interested parties have taken place. This means that a great deal of time is consumed in decision-making, but it also means that once a decision has been reached, there are few difficulties to be encountered in carrying it out. Everyone has participated, so everyone collaborates.

Can the Japanese QC circles be transplanted to North America? The evidence suggests that it can. Although inspectors in American television factories characteristically have to reject a high percentage of sets as defective, the San Diego branch of Sony, under Japanese management, was able, through use of QC circles, to achieve a 200-day record of defect-free production, a record that was superior even to Sony's factories back in Japan. Robert E. Cole, sociologist at the Center for Japanese Studies of the University of Michigan, reports that defects at Lockheed's huge operation in Sunnyvale, California, declined two thirds, after QC circles were introduced, and that worker morale and job satisfaction also improved. The savings, over a three-year period, amounted to $3 million.

Cole points out, however, that there are three conditions that will make difficulties for anyone desiring to introduce QC circles to American industrial plants: (1) the antagonism of labor unions to any form of direct collaboration between management personnel and rank-and-file employees; (2) the strong possibility that the method will be sabotaged by middle managers who view it as a threat to their traditional power and authority; and (3) the reluctance of American firms to make long-term, unconditional commitments to workers, thus blocking the kind of dedication that is needed to make QC circles work.[4]

*   *   *

The fact that QC circles have been employed with success at Sony/San Diego and at Lockheed indicates that the stumbling blocks identified by Cole may not pose insurmountable obstacles. But whether the QC circle, or any other type of group-decision approach, is successfully introduced in an organization will depend on the existence of a favorable climate of opinion. And the psychological climate of an organization is, as we have noted, influenced more by the attitudes and values of top management than by any other group. Thus the question of whether steps will be taken to humanize interpersonal relations and encourage personal involvement in an organization's goals depend on those who make its policies.

We have suggested group-decision practices as the ideal and at the same time the most practical approach to the task of improving human relations and morale in an organization or group, not only because it embodies all the principles we have discussed but also because it can serve as an effective vehicle to programs designed to change attitudes and policies that interfere with effective operations. It is a useful answer to the question: "All right, I am convinced that we need to improve human relations in this organization, but where do we start?" By laying plans to introduce the group-decision method, by preparing group members and staff to adjust their viewpoint to this important change, and by actually putting the method into practice, the emotional climate and morale of a group or organization should not only be changed for the better, but should be placed on a sounder basis.

If a group or organization has been operating on principles that are quite different from those that are implied in the group-decision method, it is quite likely that its introduction will meet with the resistance and hostility of people at all levels of responsibility and authority from the lowest to the highest, partly because any major change in procedure arouses anxieties, but also because the principles of human relations, as we have outlined them, run counter to so many prevailing practices. This is a difficulty that we have discussed before (see particularly the story of Sam Raton and the White River Furniture Company in Chapter 9), and it is a difficulty that we should always keep in mind. People unfortunately find it all too easy to give off-hand agreement to the principles of human relations and then discover,when a program is actually put into practice, that they must give up pet theories or change comfortable but ineffective ways of doing things. Such a discovery inevitably leads to a display of defensive tactics and actions aimed at sabotaging the new program. This unanticipated gap between theory and actual practice has caused the failure of countless attempts to humanize the relationship between management and workers, between leaders and their subordinates.

If those who are attempting to introduce QC circles or other group-decision methods do their homework and prepare the ground adequately, much of this after-the-fact hostility can be avoided. Introducing fundamental changes in psychological climate, patterns of thought and behavior, and leader-follower relations is best done slowly, with total participation of all who will be affected by the new ways of doing things. The slow pace of these deliberations may frustrate those who are eager to see the interpersonal and intergroup relations in an organization placed on a sound psychological basis, but it is a price that must be paid, if the changes are to endure.

But the price is worth it. There is more at stake then merely the development of better working relations in a group or organization. Improved human relations and higher morale are like a tonic. They not only affect the relations of people *on* the job or *in* the group, but they also influence their lives *outside* the group. The person who discovers that he is understood, accepted, and respected in *one* area of life, develops a new adequacy that helps him in his relationships in *other* areas of life. Because he works in an atmosphere characterized by mutual confidence, freedom, and high morale, he will be inclined to carry over some of this feeling and some of the ways he has learned to deal with others into his relations with people off the job or away from his group. And *these people* in turn, because of this influence, will find themselves better prepared to employ the principles of sound human relations in dealing with *their* associates.

Thus the benefits that result from improved human relations in one group or organization are spread through the community and out into the world. Therefore the opportunities that leaders have to make themselves more effective and develop better human relations are also their opportunities to help their organization, their community, and the world to develop better ways of living and working together.

FOOTNOTES CHAPTER 14

[1]*The Human Organization: Its Management and Value*; McGraw-Hill, 1967.

[2]*Science and Human Behavior*, Macmillan, 1953.

[3]*Psychology in Industrial Organizations*, 4th edition; Houghton Mifflin, 1973.

[4]C. Holden, Innovation: Japan Races Ahead as U.S. Falters, *Science*, 1980, vol. 210, pp. 751-754.

Bibliography

Almond, G.A., & Verba, S. *The Civic Culture: Political attitudes in five nations.* Princeton: Princeton University Press, 1963.

Bandura, A. *Social learning theory.* Englewood Cliffs, N.J.: Prentice-Hall, 1977.

Bass, B.M. *Leadership, psychology, and organizational behavior.* New York: Harper, 1960.

Bass, B.M., & Dunteman, G.H. Behavior in groups as a function of self-interaction, and task orientation. *Journal of Abnormal & Social Psychology*, 1963, vol. 66, pp. 419-428.

Beer, M. *Leadership, employee needs, and motivation.* Ohio State University, Bureau of Business Research, Monograph No. 129, 1966.

Combs, A.W., & Snygg, D. *Individual behavior*, rev. ed. New York: Harper, 1959.

Drucker, P.F. How to be an employee. *Fortune*, 1952, vol. 45 (May), pp. 126-127.

Dubin, R., Homans, G.C., Mann, F.C., & Miller, D.C. *Leadership and productivity.* San Francisco: Chandler, 1965.

Fiedler, F.E. *A theory of leadership effectiveness.* New York: McGraw-Hill, 1967.

Gintner, G., & Lindskold, S. Rate of participation and expertise as factors in influencing leader choice. *Journal of Personality & Social Psychology*, 1975, vol. 32, pp. 1085-1089.

Hawley, C. *Executive suite.* Boston: Houghton Mifflin, 1952.

Herzberg, F.I. *Work and the nature of man.* New York: World, 1966.

Holden, C. Innovation: Japan races ahead as U.S. falters. *Science*, 1980, vol. 210, pp. 751-754.

Hulin, C.L., & Blood, M.R. Job enlargement, individual differences, and worker responses. *Psychological Bulletin*, 1968, vol. 69, pp. 41-55.

Katz, D., & Kahn, R.L. *The social psychology of organizations*, 2nd ed. New York: Wiley, 1978.

Lewin, K., Lippitt, R., & White, R.K. Patterns of aggression behavior in experimentally created "social climates." *Journal of Social Psychology*, 1939, vol. 10, pp. 271-299.

Likert, R. *The human organization*. New York: McGraw-Hill, 1967.

Likert, R., & Likert, J.G. *New ways of managing conflict*. New York: McGraw-Hill, 1976.

Lindgren, H.C. *Great expectations: The psychology of money*. Los Altos, Calif.: Wm. Kaufmann, 1980.

Lindgren, H.C., & Harvey, J.H. *An introduction to social psychology*, 3rd ed. St. Louis: Mosby, 1981.

Machiavelli, N. *The prince*. New York: New American Library, 1952.

Maier, N.R.F. *Principles of human relations*. New York: Wiley, 1952.

Maier, N.R.F. *Psychology in industrial organizations*, 4th ed. Boston: Houghton Mifflin, 1973.

Roethlisberger, F.J. *Management and morale*. Cambridge: Harvard University Press, 1941.

Roethlisberger, F.J., & Dickson, W.J. *Management and the worker*. Cambridge: Harvard University Press, 1939.

Rogers, C.R. *Client-centered therapy*. Boston: Houghton Mifflin, 1951.

Schoeck, H. *Envy: A theory of social behavior*. New York: Harcourt, Brace, Jovanovich, 1970.

Servan-Schreiber, J.J. *The American challenge*. New York: Atheneum, 1979.

Shaw, M.E. *Group dynamics: The psychology of small group behavior*, 2nd ed. New York: McGraw-Hill, 1976.

Skinner, B.H. *Science and human behavior*. New York: Macmillan, 1953.

Sorrentino, R.M. & Boutillier, R.G. The effect of quantity and quality of verbal interaction on the ratings of leadership ability. *Journal of Experimental Social Psychology*, 1975, vol. 11, pp. 403-411.

Stogdill, R.M. *Handbook of leadership*. New York: Free Press, 1974.

Toffler, A. *Future shock*. New York: Random House, 1970.

Tubbs, S.L., & Widgery, R.N. When productivity lags, check at the top: Are key managers really communicating? *Management Review*, 1978, vol. 67 (Nov.), pp. 20-25.

Vroom, V.H. *Work and Motivation*. New York: Wiley, 1964.

Zander, A. *Groups at work*. San Francisco: Jossey-Bass, 1977.

Index